W9-CKR-168

# Coaching
# TRAINING

Includes CD-ROM with Ready-to-Use Microsoft PowerPoint® Presentations

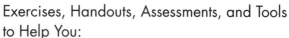

Exercises, Handouts, Assessments, and Tools to Help You:

✔ Create Coaching Programs That Build Four Key Skills: Guiding, Teaching, Motivating, and Mentoring
✔ Develop Training for Both Individual and Organizational Needs
✔ Become a More Effective and Efficient Facilitator
✔ Ensure Training Is on Target and Gets Results

**ASTD**

*Linking People, Learning & Performance*

## Chris W. Chen

**ASTD Press** is an internationally renowned source of insightful and practical information on workplace learning and performance topics, including training basics, evaluation and return-on-investment (ROI), instructional systems development (ISD), e-learning, leadership, and career development.

Ordering Information: Books published by ASTD Press can be purchased by visiting our website at store.astd.org or by calling 800.628.2783 or 703.683.8100.

Library of Congress Catalog Card Number: 2002112528

ISBN: 978-1-56286-344-9

*Acquisitions and Development Editor:* Mark Morrow
*Copyeditor:* Rick Ludwick, UpperCase Publication Services, Ltd.
*Interior Design and Production:* Christine Cotting, UpperCase Publication Services, Ltd.
*Cover Design:* Charlene Osman
*Cover Illustration:* Todd Davidson

# The ASTD Trainer's WorkShop Series

The ASTD Trainer's WorkShop Series is designed to be a practical, hands-on road map to help you quickly develop training in key business areas. Each book in the series offers all the exercises, handouts, assessments, structured experiences, and ready-to-use presentations needed to develop effective training sessions. In addition to easy-to-use icons, each book in the series includes a companion CD-ROM with PowerPoint presentations and electronic copies of all supporting material featured in the book.

Other books in the Trainer's WorkShop Series:

- *New Supervisor Training*
  John E. Jones and Chris W. Chen

- *Customer Service Training*
  Maxine Kamin

- *Leading Change Training*
  Jeffrey Russell and Linda Russell

- *Leadership Training*
  Lou Russell

- *New Employee Orientation Training*
  Karen Lawson

- *Project Management Training*
  Bill Shackelford

- *Innovation Training*
  Ruth Ann Hattori and Joyce Wycoff

- *Sales Training*
  Jim Mikula

- *Communication Skills Training*
  Maureen Orey and Jenni Prisk

- *Diversity Training*
  Cris Wildermuth with Susan Gray

- *Strategic Planning Training*
  Jeffrey Russell and Linda Russell

# C o n t e n t s

When I was presented with the opportunity to write this book my first reaction was less than enthusiastic. The term "coaching" has recently become ubiquitous in corporate America and is used in so many varied contexts it seemed that the topic would be hard to corral into a coherent and practical workbook. After some consideration, I decided to accept the project and include in it a workable definition of "coaching" described by four of the key roles coaches are expected to fulfill: guide, motivator, teacher, and mentor.

Organizing the book in this manner is intended to allow trainers to easily focus their training efforts on the specific needs of their participants and avoid the distraction that is often associated with the ambiguity concerning the role of "coach."

The training modules presented in this workbook will facilitate the alignment of expectations of the organization, supervisor, coach, and person being coached and provide a practical context for coaching.

This workbook contains a number of original structured experiences and instruments that were conceived and developed specifically for this book. However, they are broadly applicable and I hope you find them useful in a wide variety of circumstances.

I am very appreciative of the support and assistance of the professionals that helped produce this book. Mark Morrow of ASTD was instrumental in conceptualizing this work. Rick Ludwick of Uppercase Publication Services provided diligence, guidance, and a keen eye during the editing process.

I also offer thanks to my wife, Bridget, who puts up with much unwanted coaching; to my father, Richard, a devout man of God who has been my coach in many ways; and to my daughter, Jasmine, to whom I hope I am a helpful (and appreciated) coach.

During the production of this work, John E. Jones—with whom I co-authored the first in this series of workbooks, *New Supervisor Training*—passed away. He was a good friend and fountain of knowledge and contributed greatly to this book. His contributions to the field of organization development have helped many practitioners, and he will be very fondly remembered by myself and the many others who had the privilege of knowing him.

Chris W. Chen
San Diego, California
May 2003

# Introduction: How to Use This Book Effectively

**What's in This Chapter?**

- ◆ A practical definition of coaching

- ◆ Common issues coaches face

- ◆ How to use this workbook most effectively

## What Is Coaching?

In general, coaching is helping someone else expand and apply his or her skills, knowledge, and abilities. It generally takes place within a defined context, such as a specific task, skill, or responsibility.

This definition of coach covers a wide range of activities. The role of a coach might involve being a subject matter expert in a particular discipline. Or it could mean being a motivator whose pep talks and words of encouragement inspire others to greatness. It can also mean helping others set goals or find a direction for their efforts. Coaching might also be developing and maintaining an ongoing developmental relationship with one or more of the organization's rising young stars. Preparing someone to be a coach can mean training him or her in one, all, or any combination of these roles.

For the purposes of this workbook, coaching is defined as helping others succeed through guiding, teaching, motivating, and mentoring.

## Why This Is Important

There are many ways to become a coach. Indeed, you might say, "all roads lead to coaching" because the broad definition of coaching covers such a ubiquitous set of skills that we all need to coach someone on something at some point. Done well, coaching can transfer knowledge on a just-in-time basis in our organizations, increase individual motivation and morale, and help organizations deliver outstanding results. Done poorly, coaching can waste the time of valuable resources, create a hostile work environment, and create suboptimal organizations. This book facilitates the accelerated development and effective delivery of training in order to prepare participants to perform their various coaching roles effectively.

## How the Book Was Developed

The author reviewed the available literature on the subject of coaching training, interviewed other experts in the field, and combined this knowledge with his extensive array of experience in the design and delivery of interactive training that "hits the mark." The author has led numerous seminars and developmental sessions for people with coaching responsibilities, a background that enriches the contents of this book.

## The Context of the Training

The materials and designs in this book lend themselves to a broad array of organizations, both public and private. The training materials focus on helping coaches properly define their coaching roles and then develop the skills necessary for those roles. The book is designed to train people for one-on-one coaching situations. However, with little or no adjustment many of the approaches and principles also apply to group or team coaching.

## The Content of the Training

The many definitions of coaching have resulted in the overuse of the word "coach" and have created a wide range of expectations for those who take on the role of coach. There is often ambiguity concerning the role of the coach and the desired results of the coaching process. The expectations of the organization, supervisor, coach, and person being coached may be quite different. This confusion surrounding the term "coach" has increased the difficulty of training coaches.

Another issue in some organizations is that the need for coaching has become associated with having a performance problem. Coaching sessions or the coaching process are perceived as something to which poor performers are subjected so they can raise their performance to acceptable levels. This pejorative perception of the term "coaching" might limit the appeal and audience of training on the subject of coaching. Defining the role of the coach and clearly identifying desired outcomes for each coaching situation so each involved party has common expectations can mitigate these issues.

The training designs in this workbook are intended to address these concerns. The content modules in chapter 10 are divided into basic skills required by all coaching roles and skills specific to particular coaching roles.

## BASIC SKILLS

◆ **Content Module 10–1: Learning Partners.** This module helps create a collaborative learning environment by introducing participants to each other and to the idea that their roles are to contribute to the learning process.

◆ **Content Module 10–2: What Is Coaching?** The term "coaching" covers a wide variety of topics. This module covers the importance of properly defining the coaching role.

◆ **Content Module 10–3: Coaching Self-Assessment.** This module helps participants assess the topics on which they are qualified to coach and their coaching strengths and weaknesses. The module also explores how bad coaching can negatively affect performance.

◆ **Content Module 10–4: Needs Assessment and Defining the Coaching Relationship.** Agreeing with the person you are coaching on the role of the coach and the expected outcomes of the coaching process is important to a successful coaching relationship. This module covers the two-way nature of the relationship and how to align the expectations of everyone involved. It also includes an assessment to help with this process.

◆ **Content Module 10–5: Building Trust and Rapport.** The principles and techniques of building trust are included in this module.

◆ **Content Module 10–6: Listening for Understanding.** This module looks at ways to actively listen to the person being coached.

◆ **Content Module 10–7: Giving Effective Feedback.** This module explores ways to observe and deliver credible feedback.

### *SPECIFIC COACHING ROLES*

◆ **Content Module 10–8: Coach as Guide.** Helping the person being coached define and measure outcomes is the subject of this module. This includes setting goals and planning action.

◆ **Content Module 10–9: Coach as Motivator.** Does the person being coached want to succeed? What are the consequences if he or she does or does not succeed? What role does confidence or overconfidence play? The subjects of motivation and confidence are addressed in this module.

◆ **Content Module 10–10: Coach as Teacher.** This module covers how the coach can effectively transfer knowledge to another person.

◆ **Content Module 10–11: Coach as Mentor.** What is the proper role of a mentor? What is the goal of the mentoring relationship? This module looks at the role of a coach who has an ongoing mentoring relationship with someone.

## The Probable Realities of Participants

Most participants in a coaching role have common issues. The assessment process will provide specific information for a particular group of participants or for a specific organization. However, the following issues are present in many coaching situations, and awareness of them may help the trainer in designing and facilitating a training program on coaching.

◆ **The need to coach is part of the participant's general supervisory responsibilities to improve the performance of others.** This is the most common context for the word "coaching" in most organizations.

◆ **The participants have received a specific assignment to help someone else.** Their coaching roles are temporary and have a relatively well-defined scope.

◆ **The participants may not have a clear understanding of the desired outcomes of the coaching.** The term "coaching" is used to refer to a wide variety of behaviors. This can result in ambiguous expectations on the part of the coach, the person being coached, supervisors, and anyone else involved.

◆ **Participants may not want to be a coach.** Coaching doesn't appeal to everyone. Some people see it as a position warranting respect and prestige. Others see it as a waste of their time or don't feel qualified to coach.

◆ **The participants may not have had training to be a coach.** Coaching is often viewed as a naturally occurring skill. People are often asked to coach without receiving training on how to coach. It's a great sign that participants are attending coaching training, but they may have had none prior to the program.

◆ **Some participants may not have the time to be a coach.** Often, people who are asked to coach someone else are high performers. As high performers, they typically have significant, critical, and time-consuming roles. Even if they want to coach, they may not have the time.

◆ **The participants may not have any clear incentive to coach.** Few organizations provide rewards specifically tied to coaching activities.

◆ **Some participants may be coaching direct reports.** Problems arise when supervisors coach people who report directly to them. These are related to organizational performance pressures on the supervisor and defensive feelings on the part of the person being coached.

◆ **The term "coaching" has a negative connotation in some organizations.** The perception may exist that if you need coaching it's because you have a performance problem. In these organizations the coach may face resistance to the coaching efforts.

◆ **Participants assigned specific coaching assignments were probably selected because they were perceived to have technical or business or organizational skills or experience from which someone else would benefit.** This perception may or may not be true.

◆ **Participants assigned specific coaching assignments typically are not selected for their coaching skills.** However, those skills can be learned!

## How to Use This Book

The best use of this resource is to develop and conduct training sessions on the subject of improving the effectiveness of coaches. Both experienced and novice trainers will be able to use this book in a flexible manner to ensure that their sessions meet the real needs of their client organizations.

Sample training designs are included in this book, along with the materials they require. The individual content modules, structured experiences, assessments, and training instruments in this book can also be incorporated into training already offered or "mixed and matched" into a variety of custom designs.

The author strongly suggests that you

- ◆ identify your target audience for coaching training

- ◆ assess the learning needs of potential participants

- ◆ modify the enclosed designs, if necessary, or develop new ones

- ◆ evaluate the outcomes of the participants' training sessions in order to engage in continuous improvement of themselves as trainers and of the training sessions.

This book can be a reference from which you can borrow the structured experiences, instruments, assessments, and designs that fit your specific needs. A comprehensive set of steps that offer the promise of creating the maximum value in using the book appear at the end of this chapter under the heading "What to Do Next."

## The Book's Organization

This resource contains numerous individual items that can be combined in many training designs for coaches. Here are the major sets of materials.

- ◆ **Methods and effective practices** in assessing the learning needs of actual or potential training participants (chapter 2).

- ◆ **Evaluation methods and effective practices** for coaching training sessions, including assessment of the trainer and continuous-improvement approaches (chapter 5).

- ◆ **Content modules** that are either ready to use as is or to be modified to meet specific needs (chapter 10).

- ♦ **Assessments and training instruments** that address several vital dimensions of coaching effectiveness (chapter 11 and CD).

- ♦ **Structured experiences** on a variety of topics relevant to training coaches (chapter 12 and CD).

- ♦ **Microsoft Word documents** to assist in customizing the participant materials (CD).

- ♦ **Microsoft PowerPoint presentations** to assist trainers in making presentations and giving instructions (CD).

- ♦ **Bibliography** of additional resources that can support coaching training.

The aims of this book are to instruct and equip trainers with the tools to design and conduct highly interactive, engaging training for coaches that is clearly "on target."

## Icons

**Assessment:** Appears when an agenda or learning activity includes an assessment, and it identifies each assessment presented.

**CD:** Indicates materials included on the CD accompanying this workbook.

**Clock:** Indicates recommended timeframes for specific activities.

**Discussion Questions:** Points out questions you can use to explore significant aspects of the training.

**Handout:** Indicates handouts that you can print or copy and use to support training activities.

**Key Point:** Alerts you to key points that you should emphasize as part of a training activity.

**PowerPoint Slide:** Indicates PowerPoint presentations and slides that can be used individually. These presentations and slides are on the CD included with this workbook, and copies of the slides are included at the end of chapter 9. Instructions for using PowerPoint slides and the CD are included in the appendix.

 **Structured Experience:** Introduces structured experiences, which are included in chapter 12.

 **Training Instrument:** Identifies specific tools, checklists, and assessments that are used before, during, and following the training workshop.

 **What to Do Next:** Highlights recommended actions that you can take to make the transition from one section of this workbook to the next or from a specific training activity to another within a training module.

 ## What to Do Next

- ◆ Study the entire contents of the book to get an overview of the resources it contains.

- ◆ Review the contents of the accompanying compact disc so that you can understand how they relate to the material in the printed book. Open the files in Microsoft Word, PowerPoint, and Adobe Acrobat Reader so you are able to determine how to make copies of the forms you will need to print and the presentations you may use to enrich the material. This step should include a careful reading of the document "How to Use the Contents of the CD." The document is included on the CD.

- ◆ Study and apply the strategies outlined in chapter 2, "Assessing the Learning Needs of Coaches," to ensure that your sessions with coaches are relevant and timely.

- ◆ When you have absorbed the trends you discover in your training needs assessment, proceed to chapter 3. Design your session to meet specific learning needs your potential participants have expressed. Carefully consider modifying the designs in this book as you formulate your plan for facilitating the learning of your client audience. There are sample designs in chapters 6 through 9 to use as is or to modify as your needs analysis suggests. The content modules in chapter 10 are detailed. You can plan to facilitate them as they are or modify them. Chapters 11 and 12 contain the structured experiences, assessments, and training instruments the modules require. Because each of these is also a standalone item, you can easily incorporate any or all of them into your existing training designs.

◆ Prepare to facilitate your training by studying the approaches in chapter 4. Each of your sessions should improve on the previous ones, and that chapter contains tips on how you can make sure that you learn along with your trainees. Your learning will be about becoming a highly effective facilitator. The trainees' learning will be about becoming highly effective coaches.

◆ Plan to evaluate each of your training sessions. Chapter 5 tells you why this is important and gives you steps for gaining insight into the payoffs of your coaching training. Outline the steps you will take to gather and analyze evaluation data and make modifications in your training design as a result.

♦

# Assessing the Learning Needs of Coaches

♦ Methods for needs assessment

♦ Tips to improve your assessment

♦ How to use two key assessment tools

♦ Guidelines for conducting successful focus groups

## Assessment Steps

Proper assessment of training needs is the foundation of a successful and effective training program. Start by answering the following questions:

♦ **Is training really the issue?** The first step in assessing coaching needs is to determine if the apparent deficiency in coaching is truly a training issue. Organizations often turn to training as a solution without determining the root cause of a symptom or problem. Before you agree to offer coaching training, consider other possible causes of the coaching deficiency, such as poorly designed business processes, inadequate or unaligned reward and recognition systems, or improper supervision.

♦ **What behaviors need to change?** If training is found to be an appropriate solution to the root cause, the next step is to determine which behaviors need to change. What do coaches need to stop doing, start doing, or do differently?

♦ **Who needs to be trained?** There are many people in organizations who perform coaching roles. Those with supervisory roles or specific coaching assignments are the most obvious candidates. However, anyone who needs to transfer knowledge to someone else, encourage another person, or act as an informal mentor can also benefit from improving his or her coaching skills. In most organizations almost everyone performs a coaching role at some point.

♦ **How can their behavior be changed?** The fourth step is to determine how best to change the assessed behaviors. Do the coaches need additional skills? Do they lack understanding of organizational norms related to coaching or does the training need to address their attitudes toward coaching?

The following methods and tools can help you complete the assessment process.

## Methods

There are basically four discrete strategies for determining what coaches need to learn.

♦ **Survey.** This is a paper-and-pencil or intranet method of gathering information from a large or geographically dispersed group of newly named coaches. This method has the advantages of speed of data collection, objectivity, repeatability, and ease of analysis. As reality checks on coaches' learning needs, so-called 360-degree or multirater assessments are often preferable to simple self-assessments.

♦ **Individual interviews.** This strategy involves talking either face-to-face or by telephone with prospective trainees. It has the advantages of personal interface and the opportunity to achieve clarity in responses, but it is time consuming. Data from interviews—even highly structured ones—often is difficult to analyze.

♦ **Focus groups.** Structured discussion sessions with multiple participants can provide a rich source of assessment information. The group format allows participants to hear, react to, and build on the thoughts of others.

♦ **Organizational analysis.** The behavioral norms, history, and formal policies of an organization create a culture that can imply the areas in which coaches need to excel in order to realize the organization's desired purpose. This strategy includes careful study of the organization's culture, vision, purpose, mission, values, and goals.

♦ **Mixed methods.** Seldom is it desirable to employ only one of the discrete strategies to assess the learning needs of coaches. Trainers need to adopt a strategy that offers the promise of uncovering the needed competencies of coaches now and for the future of the organization. Some combination of these strategies offers the greatest likelihood of finding the real developmental needs.

## Assessment Tips

Assessing the learning needs of coaches should be carried out in a thoughtful, sensitive, and involving manner. Here are some tips, based on many years of experience.

- ◆ **Go directly to the source.** Trainers often solicit information about the learning needs of coaches from their managers. The flaws in this practice are, first, that the managers may not observe the coaching directly and; second, if their managers are the sole source of data about their learning needs, the coaches may not feel involved in any meaningful way. They may even feel threatened at the prospect of being rated by their managers. The best information comes directly from the person to be coached.

- ◆ **Only assess needs you can meet.** Training needs assessment raises expectations. It can be a message to coaches: The organization expects you to be competent in these areas. If you ask about the degree to which coaches need to be competent in building trust, you are signaling that this is important and that the organization is prepared to provide training in it.

- ◆ **Involve coaches directly.** Sometimes people don't see a need to participate in training. They see coaching as simple and straightforward. Trainers need to assess needs, but also to prepare coaches so they "buy into" training. Asking about their needs and then listening carefully is an excellent method for accomplishing both of these goals. "To what degree would you like to learn how to [____] more effectively?" "To what degree would you seriously consider participating in training to improve your competency in [____]?"

- ◆ **Make the identified needs an obvious part of your training design.** Trainees need to be able to see that they have influenced the selection of content and emphasis in the training session. A good practice is to summarize briefly the trends in the training needs assessment as you introduce the goals of the session.

◆ **Training is not a "silver bullet."** Sometimes a particular coach needs assistance, counseling, or consulting. These are best carried out one-on-one and should be completely customized to each coach's realities. If the only development opportunities afforded that person are training and attending the "school of hard knocks," much of what the person learns may miss the target.

## Two Key Resources

Chapter 11 of this sourcebook contains two useful tools that trainers can use to assess the developmental needs of coaches. Adapt either or both according to local requirements.

◆ **Assessment 11–1: Structured Interview Protocol for Assessing the Learning Needs of Coaches.** Adapt this note-taking form to reflect the parameters within which your new coach training will take place. The Word file is included on the CD that accompanies this book.

◆ **Assessment 11–2: Coaching Self-Assessment.** Use this assessment as either a training tool or as advance work for the training session. You may also adapt the instrument for 360-degree assessments. Edit the Word file on the CD that accompanies this book.

## Using Focus Groups in Training Needs Assessment

An efficient method for gathering data on the learning needs of coaches is to assemble them in groups to discuss areas in which they want help. It is important to bear in mind that focus groups can be "slippery"—that is, they can go off track easily. Participants can begin to complain about the "system" or they may want to talk about almost anything but their personal deficiencies as coaches. That is why structuring focus groups is desirable. Also, it is difficult to capture the data when several participants are speaking rapidly. We use stenographic services for this function.

Here is a step-by-step method you can adapt to prepare for and conduct effective focus groups to assess the developmental needs of coaches.

◆ Determine the "target audience" for your training. You will need the name, nature of coaching role, and contact information for each person.

◆ Schedule one or more focus group sessions in accessible, private venues. Allow about an hour for each session.

◆ Invite these people to register to attend one or more focus groups to talk about being a coach and the challenges they face in that job. Plan the groups to have five to seven members each, so every participant has a chance to talk freely and so you can efficiently capture what they say.

◆ Print sufficient copies of the Assessment 11–3: Needs Assessment Focus Group Discussion Sheet (chapter 11, page 130) and bring along writing instruments for the session.

◆ As the group convenes, greet each person. Then introduce yourself and have them introduce themselves by following this outline, which you may want to write on a poster or whiteboard:

   ◆ name

   ◆ job title

   ◆ length of service in their coaching roles

   ◆ what's going well in their coaching roles

   ◆ what chronic headaches are being encountered with their coaching roles.

◆ Pass out copies of Assessment 11–3 and ask the participants to complete it candidly. Explain that you will collect the sheets at the end of the meeting and that they should not write their names on the sheets.

◆ When all members have completed the sheets, explain that they can make changes on them any time during the discussion if they wish. (*Tip:* Don't ask, "Is everyone finished?" No one can answer that question. Instead, ask, "Does anyone need more time?")

◆ Proceed around the room with question one on the sheet. Make sure you understand what is being said. Paraphrase often, ask for examples, and probe for specifics. Ask the group what the members have in common in response to the question.

◆ Proceed in similar fashion through the remaining questions. Vary the order in which the participants respond, beginning with a different person each time.

◆ After all questions have been discussed, ask the group members to summarize what they are hearing as common themes.

◆ Test the accuracy of your recording of what was said and make corrections if necessary. Do not name names in your summary.

◆ Collect the copies of the discussion sheet.

◆ Remind participants that you will be using the information to shape the training they will be invited to attend. If the training has been scheduled, give each person a copy of a printed schedule.

◆ Thank everyone for participating.

# Designing Interactive Training for Coaches

- Basic principles of experiential learning

- Ideas for creating successful trainings

- Training design tips

## Principles of Design in Experiential Learning

The foundation for delivering effective coaching training is a well-conceived design. An appropriate design considers both the abilities of the facilitator and the needs of the participants. This requires carefully thinking through the learning readiness and training needs of potential participants and creating a sequence of events to maximize the possibility that they will learn what they need to learn in the time allotted. This means *designed learning,* or a structured plan for helping coaches develop the knowledge, skills, attitudes, strategies, and tactics in which they need to be competent in order to be successful. The proper design will increase the comfort of the facilitator and allow the facilitator to deliver an enjoyable and effective program with a minimum of stress.

Much has been documented about how adults learn best. As table 3–1 shows, Jones, Bearley, and Watsabaugh (1996) have pointed out several "truths" about adult learning.

Given these principles of adult learning, it is imperative to design sessions that are highly interactive and engaging. It is impossible to force anyone to learn anything, so the goal of effective training design is to provide every opportunity and encouragement to the potential learner. Involvement of the learner is the key. As an old Chinese proverb says, "Tell me and I will forget. Show me and I may remember. Involve me and I will understand." The designs in this book use several methods to convey information and

### Table 3–1

## Learning Principles and Implications for Design

| LEARNING PRINCIPLES | IMPLICATIONS FOR TRAINING DESIGN |
| --- | --- |
| The adult is a partner with the facilitator in the learning process. | Participants should actively influence the learning approach. |
| Adults are capable of taking responsibility for their own learning. | Incorporate self-directed learning activities in the session design. |
| Adult learners gain through two-way communication. | Avoid overuse of lectures and "talking-to." Emphasize discussion. |
| Adults learn through reflection on their and others' experience. | Use interactive methods such as case studies, role-playing, and so forth. |
| Adults learn what they perceive to be useful in their life situations. | Make the content and materials closely fit assessed needs. |
| Adults' attention spans are a function of their interest in the experience. | Allow plenty of time to "process" the learning activities. |
| Adults are most receptive to instruction that is clearly related to problems they face daily. | Include applications planning in each learning activity. |
| | Promote giving inquiry into problems and affirm the experience of participants. |
| Adults do not typically see themselves as learners. | Give participants a rationale for becoming involved and provide opportunities for success. |
| Adults learn better in a climate that is informal and personal. | Promote getting acquainted and interpersonal linkages. |
| Adult learners apply learning that they have been influential in planning. | Diagnose and prioritize learning needs and preferences during the session as well as before. |
| Adults learn when they feel supported in experimenting with new ideas and skills. | Use learning groups as "home bases" for participants. |
| Adults are likely to have somewhat fixed points of view that make them closed to new ways of thinking and behaving. | Include interpersonal feedback exercises and opportunities to experiment. |
| Adults learn to react to the differential status of members of the group. | Use subgroups to provide safety and readiness to engage in open interchange. |
| Adults are internally motivated to develop increased effectiveness. | Make all learner assessment self-directed. |
| Adults filter their learning through their values systems. | Provide activities that focus on cognitive, affective, and behavioral change. |

engage participants. By incorporating a variety of training mediums—such as well-designed overhead presentations, discussion sessions, small-group work, structured exercises, and self-assessments—these designs maximize active participant involvement and offer something for every learning style.

In addition to engaging the interest of the learner, interactive training allows you to tap into another source of learning content: the participants themselves. Everyone knows something about coaching. Each of us acts as a coach to someone in some venue in our lives (for example, coaching a children's soccer team, teaching a friend to fish, helping someone fix a water heater). In a group-learning situation, a good learning environment will allow and encourage every participant to share with others in the group so the entire group's cumulative knowledge about coaching can be used.

## A Note on Training Language

This set of principles and their implications for designing experiential learning for coaches should make it clear that training is not "teaching." Trainers should not use terminology associated with education. This includes such words as the following (the training language is shown in parentheses):

- ◆ course (training session)
- ◆ instructor (facilitator)
- ◆ evaluation (assessment)
- ◆ classroom (training room or venue)
- ◆ textbook (participant material or guide).

The organizational learning experience differs greatly from most academic experiences. It is inherently more practical and targeted. Many people have negative memories of their formal schooling, so trainers should be careful not to bring these to mind in designing sessions.

## Using the Sample Designs in This Book

If you study the sample designs in chapters 6 through 9 and the content modules in chapter 10, you will discover a number of effective practices in designing interactive training for coaches. Here are the major generalizations you may draw from this study.

- **Break up the time into segments.** This applies both to brief training sessions and longer ones. First, determine the "chunks" of time you have, such as half a day or a morning.

- **Design each segment so it has a beginning, middle, and end.** Break each segment into the smaller divisions that are required for your training activities and debriefings. Structure the length of each segment on the time required for the activity; need for participant breaks; and the need of the trainer to refresh himself or herself, gather thoughts, or get organized.

- **Anticipate what training activities might take more or less time than you expect.** You may need to stay with a group discussion longer if it is particularly productive. If a structured experience goes quickly, you need to be prepared to adjust the timing of your remaining learning activities accordingly or insert another in "real time."

- **Make a seamless transition from one set of activities to the following one.** In a training session with multiple modules, it is important to make sure the participants see how each module relates and leads into the next. Your training should not feel segmented. Make transition statements that bridge the time segments: "Now that we've considered what it takes to be an effective coach in this organization, let's build on that by considering. . . . " The bridges and relationships may be obvious to the designer of the training, but it helps to point them out with meaningful segues to participants.

- **Don't short-change the debriefings.** Here is where the learning becomes crystallized and commitments are made for more effective behavior after the training. Allow plenty of time to talk through the results of each learning activity.

- **Spell out a step-by-step plan for each session.** The samples in this book give you models to consider in this regard. Sometimes your design includes activities that you and your trainees carry out after the formal session.

- **Make sure that trainees see how the pieces fit together.** You may present an overview at the beginning of your session and refer to it as you move through the sequence of learning activities that make up your design.

◆ **Consider designing a follow-up session for trainees.** If you can get the participants' commitment, plan a "booster-shot" session to take place about a month after the training session. During this meeting you can foster discussions among the participants of what worked, where they may be continuing to have difficulty, and what further training they would like to attend.

## Tips on Designing Effective Training for Coaches

Working out your plan for facilitating the learning of coaches is as much an art as a science. Your training designs implicitly express your theory of learning.

Here are some things to consider as you prepare the detailed plan for your sequence of training activities:

◆ **Begin with learning goals.** Your training needs assessment should have resulted in your having a clear understanding about what the coaches you want to train need to learn. Remember the slogan, "More than three goals are no goals" as you prepare a statement of what you hope to accomplish in your training session. Avoid getting bogged down in setting numerous objectives ("By 8:37 a.m. trainees will be able to . . ."). Don't confuse goals with activities. Goals relate to what you will purposefully explore with trainees; activities are how you plan to do that.

◆ **Pay particular attention to your beginning and ending activities.** Another saying to keep in mind is, "You never get a second chance to make a good first impression." Because it is often difficult to recover from an unfortunate beginning in training, think this through carefully. The first words you say and the first things you do are critical. At the end you want trainees to leave feeling informed, empowered, focused, and confident. Your close should emphasize their success in their next steps.

◆ **Allow plenty of time for debriefings of experiential activities.** It is tempting to emphasize the fun aspects of training activities. It is imperative that you guide participants carefully through all the steps of experiential learning—doing, sharing, looking for patterns, considering "So what?" and "Now what?" A good rule of thumb is to plan at least as much time for talking through the outcomes of a learning experience as the activity itself takes. (See chapter 4 for more on debriefing experiential activities.)

◆ **Make contingency plans.** Training sessions rarely go exactly as planned. You need to have in mind how you will respond to various events that may occur. Plan for such things as interruptions, trainees leaving and returning, fire drills, energy blackouts, and domineering participants.

◆ **Ask one or more colleagues to critique your designs before facilitating them.** You can benefit greatly from the experience of other trainers as you prepare your design. Avoid becoming defensive as they make suggestions or question your rationale. Promise them feedback on how the session turns out.

◆ **Plan to solicit the feedback you need to improve your designs.** You will not be objective in assessing how trainees react to your training. Ask them how the session might be improved. What do you need to continue, do more of, do less of, start doing, or stop doing to facilitate the design effectively? Ask one or more observers to watch the training and inform you on what needs to be changed.

Making your training pay off for both your participants and for the organization requires that you approach the design task with solid information about their learning needs and using the available resources creatively and thoughtfully.

# Facilitating Coaching Training

- A definition of the facilitator role

- The five phases of the Experiential Learning Cycle

- Questions to use in the debriefing process

- Tips on creating a learning environment

## The Role of the Facilitator

Facilitating training effectively involves being a combination of event organizer, public speaker, counselor, and entertainer.

- **Event organizer.** The effective delivery of a training program requires effective planning. Logistics regarding facilities, equipment, materials, and participants must be coordinated. Proper planning includes contingency arrangements for when things don't go according to plan. Large training departments may provide administrative help with logistics planning, but when participants arrive it's up to the facilitator to make sure everything is running smoothly. In larger groups, facilitation also involves crowd control. Getting the participants back from breaks on time and refocused on the program is a big part of creating a productive learning environment.

- **Public speaker.** When you are the facilitator the spotlight is on you. The participants look to you for behavioral cues. Your physical presence and speaking style set the tone for the program. You need to know your material so you can convey it to others. You must also be able to "think on your feet" because anything can happen in an interactive design.

- **Counselor.** Perhaps the most critical difference between a facilitator and the teachers most of us experienced as students is the listening role of the facilitator. The ability to actively listen to your participant's verbal comments and physical cues and understand their concerns and questions is the most important skill a facilitator must demonstrate. Listening intently for an extended period of time can be mentally exhausting, so be well rested and prepared.

- **Entertainer.** Few of us are good stand-up comedians and we shouldn't try to be. However, participants feed on the energy of the facilitator. A low-energy, soft-spoken, unanimated facilitator will create a low-energy program with little interaction by participants. Humor, interesting personal stories, sincere interest in the participants and subject matter and—most important—high energy make an engaging facilitator.

Planning, effective speaking, listening, and demonstrating high energy increase the effectiveness of a facilitator. However, it is also important to be yourself. Emphasize your strong points and mitigate skills or behaviors with which you are less comfortable. Do not try to be someone you are not. Use the materials in this book to design a training program well suited to your skills and personality.

## What Is a Facilitator?

There can be confusion within the training and development field about terminology used to denote persons or roles. Here are some useful distinctions:

- **Facilitator.** From the French word "facile," or "easy," facilitation is the art and science of assisting learners in experiencing content. Because the facilitator role is the subject of this chapter, this distinction will become more clear later. Facilitation typically occurs in organizational meetings and training sessions.

- **Educator.** This is a person who "teaches," or disseminates knowledge and understanding to "students" or "pupils." The educator, or teacher, operates in classroom and laboratory settings, leading students from a position of authority and superior knowledge. In training and development terms, many educators play the role of subject matter expert.

- ◆ **Trainer.** This role centers on getting trainees "up to speed" on competencies. The trainer is able to specify what excellence looks like in the area in which trainees are working. The focal points are specific job-task knowledge, skills, and effective practices. Trainers typically operate in training rooms, with groups of "trainees."

- ◆ **Counselor.** Providing private, confidential assistance to employees on personal problems can be a useful professional service. This role requires specialized education and training, however, and not all training-and-development practitioners are qualified to engage in this activity.

- ◆ **Consultant.** This role emphasizes working with employees, such as new coaches, in a partnership arrangement. Consultants help "clients" analyze situations that need attention, explore and evaluate options, and commit to action plans. There are two basic types of consulting—expert and process. Experts give clients advice; process-oriented consultants help clients learn how to improve work processes, including interpersonal ones.

The facilitator, then, works with learners in a manner that helps them open themselves to new learning and makes the process easy. The role requires that you avoid projecting yourself as a subject matter expert and that you set up activities that foster learning through "hands-on" experience and interaction. Major aspects of excellence in facilitation are setting up proper experiential learning activities or "exercises," and "processing" or leading discussions of the results. The latter activity is often referred to as "debriefing."

## Experiential Learning

Jones and Pfeiffer (1985) developed the Experiential Learning Cycle, which guides much of what is included in this book. As shown in Figure 4–1, the cycle demonstrates graphically the importance of facilitation of activity-based learning.

- ◆ **Experiencing** is the activity phase of experiential learning. It involves learners engaging in a common learning activity that provides the basis for extrapolation to the "real world." For example, everything that precedes the debriefing in the exercises in this workbook could be thought of as experiencing.

*Figure 4–1*

**The Five Phases of the Experiential Learning Cycle**

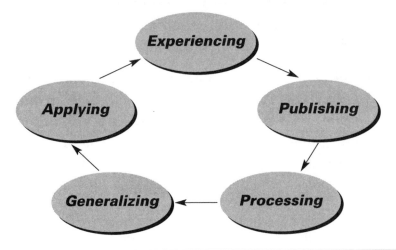

- ◆ **Publishing** involves learners sharing what they experienced and observed during the learning activity, or Experiencing, phase. This sharing may consist of feelings, thoughts, and reactions to each other's behavior. This constitutes the "raw data" from which learning can be abstracted through the next two steps of the cycle.

- ◆ **Processing** is group discussion of the dynamics of the learning activity. The search here is for commonalities, trends, and other patterns within the data set flushed out by the Publishing step. Generally, the Processing step is aided by having the facilitator ask questions that begin with either "what" or "how" rather than "why."

- ◆ **Generalizing** requires moving the group discussion from "in here" to "out there." It means drawing "truths" from the common learning experience. Learners draw "So what?" conclusions. The facilitator poses questions that lead trainees to think about what seems to be true about their worlds from the discussion of their common learning experience and discussion of their reactions.

- ◆ **Applying** is discussing what was learned and committing to putting it to work. The facilitator leads learners to respond to the general question, "Now what?" The applications may focus on teams, individuals, or the organization itself. Typically, the master facilitator pushes for concrete action planning, based on what was learned in the exercise. This involves specifying what will be done, by whom, with what intent, to what extent, and exactly when. The facilitator also pushes trainees to determine what metrics they will use to track progress toward their goals.

## Debriefing Experiential Learning

As you can see, experiential learning, or participative training, requires that the trainer play the role of facilitator of learning rather than the dispenser of knowledge. The latter model can be thought of as the "sponge" approach: the trainer dispenses knowledge and the participants soak it up. Experiential learning appeals to adults because it is maximally sensitive to their experiences and insights. It also can result in broader application of learning; because trainees develop the learning for themselves, they "own" it.

Some trainers fill their sessions with activities and fail to work through the learning cycle adequately. A rule of thumb is to spend at least as much time debriefing exercises as conducting them—at least. The debriefing discussion is where participants crystallize learning that applies to their work as coaches. They develop plans to make practical applications so they can move beyond just having fun or an interesting experience.

Many training activities are inherently pleasant. Some people enjoy competitions, and others take pleasure in contemplating how relationships can help or hinder the organization's work. It is important that trainers thoroughly understand the importance of skillful debriefing of experiential learning and commit to continuous growth in their competence in playing the role of learning facilitator.

The best approach in debriefings is to keep the Experiential Learning Cycle in mind as you lead trainees from general to specific considerations. Here are representative "marker" questions that the facilitator can use to implement the cycle fully.

### EXPERIENCING

- ◆ What emotions did you experience during the activity?

- ◆ In response to what did you have these feelings?

### PUBLISHING

- ◆ How did you see yourself behaving during the exercise?

- ◆ What did you notice in the behavior of others?

- ◆ How did you react to others' behavior during the exercise?

- ◆ How did others respond to your behavior?

## *PROCESSING*

- ◆ What patterns of behavior seemed to emerge during the activity?

- ◆ What did the feelings of group members have in common?

## *GENERALIZING*

- ◆ What can we conclude from the results of this exercise?

- ◆ What seems to cause what in this type of situation?

- ◆ How does this exercise mirror what goes on in our work as coaches?

- ◆ What appear to be the costs involved in doing tasks the way we did them in this exercise?

- ◆ What would be substantially better?

- ◆ As a result of participating in this exercise . . .

  - ◆ what did you learn?

  - ◆ what did you re-learn?

  - ◆ what are you beginning to learn?

  - ◆ what do you need to learn?

## *APPLYING*

- ◆ How might we behave more effectively as coaches, given what we learned in this exercise?

- ◆ How might our coaches use what we learned in this activity to make their task and relationship behaviors more effective?

- ◆ What will you as a coach do differently as a result of what we learned in this exercise?

- ◆ When will you do it?

- ◆ How much will you do it?

- ◆ Where will you do it?

- ◆ How will you track progress on applying what you learned in this exercise?

The facilitator should, of course, adapt these questions to his or her own personality. Don't simply read them aloud. Stay in the mentality (and reality) of the coaches as you guide them all the way through to asking and answering the questions, "So what?" and "Now what?" The job of the facilitator is not to "teach" but to make the process of learning through discovery easy. You have to trust that learners, as adults, can take from experiential activities what they need.

Of course, conducting exercises and facilitating debriefings are not the only roles facilitators play in developmental sessions with new coaches. Sometimes you lecture, guide trainees through assessments, introduce subject matter experts, or host senior managers. There is more than one way to learn, but it is incumbent on facilitators to be proficient in carrying out the responsibilities of facilitating experiential learning.

## Creating the Learning Environment

A critical factor in making learning easy is the creation of a learning environment. The facilitator should seek to create four conditions to maximize learning:

- ◆ **Confidentiality.** The first step to learning is to admit ignorance. New coaches may resist admitting their learning needs because they fear the repercussions of showing their weaknesses. You can alleviate these concerns by assuring participants that the sole purpose of the training is to build their skills and that no evaluations will take place. Setting the condition that discussions and events during the training program remain confidential among the participants and facilitators will help create a risk-free environment.

- ◆ **Freedom from distractions.** Work and personal demands cannot be ignored during training, but should be minimized in order to maximize each participant's learning and as a courtesy to others. Ask that cell phones and pagers be turned off or set to inaudible alerts. Selecting a training site away from the workplace will help a great deal in reducing distractions. Acknowledge that participants don't have time to be away from work but, inasmuch as they are away, ask them to immerse themselves in the learning experience to maximize the value of their time in training.

◆ **Participants are responsible for their own learning.** The facilitator can only create the opportunity for learning. Experiential learning demands that participants be actively engaged and committed to learning. The facilitator cannot force learning on anyone. If a participant leaving a well-designed training session (which use of this book guarantees!) says, "I have learned nothing," then that statement is more a reflection on the participant than the facilitator. The facilitator's role is to create a learning environment in which participants are challenged, intrigued, and able to explore and address their own developmental needs. It is up to the participants to respond to the learning environment and, if necessary, inform the facilitator if the environment is not meeting their needs. You can lead a horse to water, but you can't make it drink.

◆ **All participants are "learning partners."** Each participant brings some relevant knowledge to the training program. A successful training session will tap into the knowledge of each participant through discussion and sharing of information. Encourage all participants to accept responsibility for helping others learn.

## What to Do Next

◆ **Plan.** Make sure you are prepared to use all of the elements of your design effectively. Plan to maximize the appropriateness of your facilitation style. What will you be working on in your approach to training? What skills do you want to sharpen while facilitating this training? How will you obtain coaching and feedback on these skills?

◆ **Practice.** Go through the training materials in your design carefully. Be prepared to respond to trainees' questions that the materials and activities might generate. Make the PowerPoint presentations to a friend or colleague in order to become comfortable with the points you want to make.

◆ **Recruit co-trainers.** You and your trainees can benefit from having co-facilitators, but more than two can be confusing and excessive. Having an experienced line manager or executive as co-trainer means that you may need to coach the person to play the role of facilitator. His or her active involvement can add greatly to the legitimacy of your training. Using subject matter experts—such as a well-known motivator or teacher—can also add depth and credibility to the delivery of your training. You will need to coach each of the subject matter experts before and after the session for maximum effectiveness and minimal surprises.

◆ **Prepare all needed materials and test your equipment.** Using the CD that accompanies this book, print enough copies of the assessments and training instruments needed in your design. Set up your computer to project the PowerPoint shows and rehearse the ones called for by your design.

# Evaluating and Improving Coaching Training

## What's in This Chapter?

- Overview of a classic evaluation method
- How to use the included instruments for your own evaluations
- Tips on interpreting and making use of evaluation results
- Steps to successful evaluation

## Why Bother?

Evaluating training can generate many benefits, both to the trainer and to the organization. Not evaluating training is like hitting golf balls into a fog: You know they land, but you don't know where. You don't know if you are hitting the ball too hard or not hard enough, or if you need to adjust your swing.

Here are the three major motivations for, and benefits of, evaluating the coaching training you design and deliver.

1. The training outcomes need to be aligned with the developmental needs you presumably have assessed. In other words, did the training deliver on the needs the coaches in your organization have at this time?

2. You can justify the continuation of investing in coaching training if you can demonstrate that it is on target.

   - Did the trainees like the training?
   - Did they learn it?
   - Did they use it?
   - Did it pay off?

3. You can adopt a scientific approach to improving the design and delivery of the training you provide for coaches. Most total quality programs emphasize making business decisions based on data. Evaluating your training carefully ensures that the continuous improvement of your training is driven by real information and not just general impressions or anecdotes.

## The Classic Levels of Training Evaluation

Kirkpatrick (1996) developed a famous model for training evaluation. It consists of four levels and guides much of the practice of measuring the outcomes of training in many countries. The levels are graduated, from the relatively easy to measure to the more complex.

1. **Reaction:** Measuring the reaction of participants to the program. This is a measure of "customer satisfaction" because those who attend are customers whose reaction determines to a large extent the interest in present and future programs.

2. **Learning:** Measuring the extent to which learning objectives have been achieved. Has knowledge increased, have skills improved or attitudes changed as a result of the program?

3. **Behavior:** Measuring the extent to which participants changed their behavior in the organization because they attended the program.

4. **Results:** Measuring the organizational results from behavioral changes that were accomplished because participants attended the program.

The least effective, but most common, evaluation method is at the first level and uses what are often called "Smile Sheets." These typically use Likert scales to answer questions regarding the effectiveness of the training content and delivery. These questions are often asked in terms of "value" and participant enjoyment of the training. Smile Sheets give an indication of the immediate reactions of participants. However, immediate reactions may have no relationship to actual learning. Tasty refreshments and an entertaining presentation can produce positive participant reactions, but may not affect learning or behavior. Also, some participants follow the old adage, "If you don't have anything nice to say, don't say anything at all." They either give high marks that don't reflect their real reactions or they don't complete the evaluation.

Smile Sheets are commonly used because they are easy to administer and can be of some value. Positive scores may not be indicative of effective training, but negative evaluations are a strong indication that the training is not effective. Also, open-ended questions that allow participants to provide comments on the training can provide important, useful feedback.

Because the four evaluation levels are ranked according to complexity, they are also, in effect, ranked according to decreasing use. That is, more organizations use Smile Sheets than attempt to measure learning. Fewer track on-the-job behavioral changes, and still fewer engage in the difficult task of specifying the return-on-investment in supervisory training. The author strongly recommends that trainers take whatever steps they need to evaluate their sessions more thoroughly. If training is to become thought of as a key business activity, trainers need to be accountable for the value they claim to add to the organization.

## Instruments for Evaluation in This Workbook

Chapter 11 of this workbook includes three instruments that lend themselves to applications of evaluating training. The first two can also be used in training designs.

◆ **Assessment 11–2: Coaching Self-Assessment.** This tool calls for coaching training participants to analyze their strengths and developmental needs. The instrument can be used not only as prework for an initial training module but also as a repeat measure either at the end of the session or sometime afterward.

◆ **Trainer Competencies.** This form, which is part of Assessment 11–2, lets you establish learning priorities for your own development. It can be used at any time, and you can use it to solicit feedback from trainees, either at the end of sessions or sometime afterward.

◆ **Assessment 11–5: Coaching Training Follow-Up Assessment.** This questionnaire should be distributed some time after the close of the coaching training. It gets at level three on the Kirkpatrick model. This instrument can be used in follow-up "reunions" of trainees or as a survey questionnaire. It can also include ratings from "significant others" in the trainees' work environments.

Trainers are not limited to using these three instruments, of course. It is important that you commit yourself to systematic evaluation and that you conduct it routinely. That way you build up an understanding of "what works" with your people.

## Improving Training for Coaches

One large contribution the total quality movement made to organizations is the concept of continuous improvement. You don't wait for technological breakthroughs or "innovation." Instead, you attend to the details of what you are doing to get work done, with an emphasis on work processes. Applied to training coaches, commitment to continuous improvement means

- ♦ specifying the steps you are taking

- ♦ analyzing the logic of the sequence

- ♦ looking carefully at the efficacy of each detailed step

- ♦ making changes that offer chances of making the training work better and better.

This approach requires you to document what you are doing and carefully evaluate the effects, or outcomes, of each step.

Paying attention to customers is also a central notion of quality. In training, this means assessing the learning needs and preferences of potential participants, involving them in evaluating the training, and providing other services to them—such as one-on-one assistance—as they apply what they learned to their work situations.

Trainers should avoid getting too attached to particular training activities. A better approach to improving training is to experiment with both the content and design. If activities do not produce desired results, either change or discontinue them. Try new ways and new activities to deliver on the same objectives.

Also, learn ways of evaluating training on more than one level. The data developed by levels two through four of Kirkpatrick's model can give you rich insight into how to improve your training of coaches. This takes more time than simply administering Smile Sheets, but the payoffs can be substantial.

When time has passed after your training, you can also solicit feedback on your competencies as a trainer and facilitator. This information can guide you through the process of developing as a professional. The root cause of less-than-optimal coaching training is often the trainer, not the design. You may be getting in the way of the effectiveness of your sessions. Asking for feedback on what you can change is a direct way of managing your growth as a trainer, but soliciting feedback is far down the list of things that coaches do naturally. They want it, but they are reluctant to ask for it. You can become their role model by actively engaging them in your own quest for excellence.

## What to Do Next

Here is a step-by-step method for maximizing the benefits of your efforts at evaluating your training sessions for coaches.

- ◆ **Decide which steps to follow.** Lay out a step-by-step plan for evaluating the outcomes (impacts, payoffs) of your training for coaches. Specify who will do what, when, how much, and for what purpose. Establish a timeline for these steps.

- ◆ **Gather feedback.** Solicit data from trainees and all relevant others. Use the instruments included in this book to assist you in this process.

- ◆ **Analyze results.** Conduct both statistical and content analyses of the responses you receive while gathering data for your evaluation. Be as objective as possible during this step because you may be predisposed to use the data to validate your own opinions and observations.

- ◆ **Modify the design as necessary.** Your evaluation program is the beginning of your design improvement process. Use the results to strengthen what is working well, and change the selection, content, or sequence of activities to reach your training objectives more effectively.

# Individual/ Small Group Session

- Advice on working with individuals and small groups

- Considerations in choosing the right content for training sessions

- Step-by-step preparation and training delivery instructions

- Sample agendas

The materials in this workbook are designed to meet a variety of training needs. They cover a range of topics related to coaches and can be offered in many different timeframes and formats. Although learning experiences can be enhanced and their depth increased by lengthy immersion in the learning environment, organizational life sometimes demands that training be done in short, small doses. Organizational size and work demands may also limit the number of participants available at any particular time. This chapter discusses session designs for training coaches individually and in small groups.

## Individual Session

### TRAINING OBJECTIVES

The objectives of an individual training session are to convey as much information as possible to the participant in a short time and build the relationship between the trainer and the participant. The one-on-one interaction between trainer and participant is the greatest advantage of individual training sessions. The participant's particular questions and issues can be explored in greater depth than in a session with multiple participants.

An individual training session is appropriate for the following circumstances:

◆   The targeted, available audience for training is one person.

◆   One individual requires training in one particular area of content.

◆   Training facilities for multiple participants are not available.

## TIME

◆   1 to 2.5 hours

### CHOOSING THE CONTENT

One of the advantages of training a single participant is the ability to select content specific to an individual need. Although all of the content modules in this book can be used for individual training, some are more easily tailored than others. The structured experiences in this book typically require multiple participants, but some exercises may be executed by a single participant working with a trainer. The content modules most appropriate for an individual training session are

◆   Content Module 10–2: What Is Coaching?

◆   Content Module 10–3: Coaching Self-Assessment

◆   Content Module 10–4: Needs Assessment and Defining the Coaching Relationship

◆   Content Module 10–6: Listening for Understanding

◆   Content Module 10–8: Coach as Guide

◆   Content Module 10–9: Coach as Motivator

◆   Content Module 10–10: Coach as Teacher

◆   Content Module 10–11: Coach as Mentor.

These modules are in chapter 10.

Although all of the modules are not readily adaptable to individual training sessions, there is enough content suitable for one-on-one training to cover a wide range of coaching issues. Your training needs assessment will help you prioritize and select the content modules of highest value for your audience.

The timing of certain topics is another thing to consider when choosing content. For instance, the "What Is Coaching?" module provides an introduction to the issues coaches face and provides a foundation for the other modules. It should be offered first if a series of modules will be presented. The "Coaching Self-Assessment" module helps to focus the learning efforts of the coach and should be offered early in the training process. The "Needs Assessment and Defining the Coaching Relationship" module helps the coach define the role he or she will play with the person being coached and is ideally offered prior to the "Coach as Guide," "Coach as Teacher," "Coach as Motivator," and "Coach as Mentor" modules.

This sample agenda is designed for someone who is beginning his or her training on coaching. It contains the "What Is Coaching?" and "Coaching Self-Assessment" modules.

## MATERIALS

*For the instructor:*

- This chapter for reference

- Content Module 10–2: What Is Coaching?

- Content Module 10–3: Coaching Self-Assessment

- Structured Experience 12–1: What Is Coaching?

- PowerPoint presentation: What Is Coaching? To access slides for this program, open the file *What Is Coaching.ppt* on the accompanying CD. Copies of the slides for this training session are included at the end of chapter 9 (slides 9–1 through 9–10).

*For the participants:*

- Assessment 11–2: Coaching Self-Assessment

## SAMPLE AGENDA

| | |
|---|---|
| 8:00 a.m. | Introductions (5 minutes) |
| 8:05 | Content Module 10–2: What Is Coaching? (chapter 10, page 99) (1 hour) |
| 9:05 | Break (10 minutes) |
| 9:15 | Content Module 10–3: Coaching Self-Assessment (chapter 10, page 100) (1 hour) |
| 10:15 | Close |

### *STEP-BY-STEP PLANNING*

*At the training session:*

- ◆ Introduce yourself to the participant. Include a description of your role in the training process and your training and work experience. First impressions count, and this is your chance to establish credibility with the participant.

- ◆ Ask the participant to introduce himself or herself to you, including his or her name, role, and coaching experience. Let the participant know this is an informal session and try to put him or her at ease.

- ◆ Review the agenda and learning objectives with the participant.

- ◆ Go through the selected content module(s).

- ◆ Take a break about an hour into the session.

- ◆ Ask for questions and test for understanding frequently.

- ◆ Close the session with an opportunity for the participant to ask questions. If appropriate, offer your help and availability on an ongoing basis.

## Small Group Session

### *TRAINING OBJECTIVES*

The objectives of a small group training session are to convey as much information as possible to the participants in a short period of time and build relationships among the trainer and the participants. The small group setting allows in-depth discussion of a limited set of issues.

A small group training session is appropriate for the following circumstances:

- ◆ The targeted training audience consists of seven people or less.

- ◆ A few individuals require training in one particular area of content.

- ◆ Training facilities for large groups are not available.

 ### *TIME*

- ◆ 1 to 2.5 hours

## *CHOOSING THE CONTENT*

Any of the content modules in this book can be used for small group training. Select the module(s) based on the needs assessment of the participant group.

This sample agenda assumes that the most pressing need for this small group is to understand how to build trust in a relationship. We've selected the "Learning Partners" and "Building Trust and Rapport" modules. The former module is an introduction exercise that helps to create the learning environment by preparing participants to act as learning partners. The latter module helps coaches define the boundaries of trust in a relationship and looks at ways to build trust between themselves and the person they are coaching.

## *MATERIALS*

*For the instructor:*

♦ This chapter for reference

♦ Content Module 10–1: Learning Partners

♦ Content Module 10–5: Building Trust and Rapport

♦ Structured Experience 12–3: Building Rapport

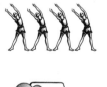

♦ Structured Experience 12–4: Trust Walk

♦ PowerPoint presentation: Building Trust and Rapport. To access slides for this program, open the file *Building Trust and Rapport.ppt* on the accompanying CD. Copies of the slides for this training session are included at the end of chapter 9 (slides 9–40 through 9–46).

## *SAMPLE AGENDA*

8:00 a.m.  Content Module 10–1: Learning Partners (chapter 10, page 98) (15 minutes)

8:15  Content Module 10–5: Building Trust and Rapport (chapter 10, page 103) (2.25 hours)

10:30  Close

### STEP-BY-STEP PLANNING

*Just before the training session:*

- ◆ Arrive early at the facility.

- ◆ Set up and test equipment (such as projectors or flipcharts).

*At the training session:*

- ◆ Introduce yourself to the participants. Include a description of your role in the training process and your training and work experience. First impressions count, and this is your chance to establish credibility with the participants.

- ◆ If you do not use the learning partners exercise, ask the participants to introduce themselves. They should include their name, role, and coaching experience. Let them know they will be helping each other learn.

- ◆ Review the agenda and learning objectives with the participants.

- ◆ Go through the selected content module(s).

- ◆ Take a break about an hour into the session.

- ◆ Ask for questions and test for understanding frequently.

- ◆ Close the session with an opportunity for the participants to ask questions. If appropriate, offer your help and availability on an on-going basis.

## What to Do Next

- ◆ Identify the training participant(s) and assess the most critical training needs.

- ◆ Determine the time available for the training session.

- ◆ Select the highest value content module(s) based on needs and on time available.

- ◆ Schedule the session.

- ◆ Arrange a facility for the training session.

- ◆ Invite the participant(s).

◆ Send a confirmation to participants. Include an agenda and any advance work with the confirmation.

◆ Prepare training materials (handouts, overheads, presentations).

# Half-Day Session

- Advice on choosing the content for training sessions
- Step-by-step preparation and training delivery instructions
- Sample agendas

The materials included in this book can be used for a variety of training needs and timeframes. This chapter covers designs suitable for half-day (four-hour) training sessions. Group training is generally more effective and enjoyable than one-on-one training sessions and should be used whenever possible. The learning environment is enhanced by contributions from a variety of participants. Although group learning dynamics can be obtained with as few as 3 participants, groups of between 12 and 24 participants are the most conducive to a learning environment.

## Objectives and Use

The objectives of a half-day training session are to build understanding of the learning content that is of greatest value to the organization and the participants and build relationships between the trainer and the participants. The group setting allows for rich and diverse discussion of the various topics.

A half-day training session is appropriate for the following circumstances:

- The targeted, available audience for training is three or more.
- The targeted audience requires training in several areas of content.
- Training facilities for groups are available.
- The time available for the training session is limited to four hours.

## Choosing the Content

Any of the content modules in this book can be used for half-day training sessions. Select the modules based on the needs assessment of the participant group. If the participant group does not have an identified set of assessed needs (an assessment was not completed or an open registration process is being used), select the modules based on the competencies the organization seeks to develop.

The entire curriculum contained in this book can be offered in a series of half-day sessions. The order of certain topics should be considered when selecting which content will be offered first. As noted in the previous chapter, the "What Is Coaching?" and "Coaching Self-Assessment" modules should be offered early in the training process. The sample designs in this chapter include these modules in the first of several half-day sessions that together cover all of the book's content modules.

*A note:* When your training session is at least a half-day long, you've crossed the refreshment threshold. Hunger and thirst are enemies to the learning environment, so offer drinks and snacks at the breaks so your participants' biological needs are met.

For the first sample agenda, we've selected the "What Is Coaching?" "Coaching Self-Assessment," and "Needs Assessment and Defining the Coaching Relationship" modules.

## Sample Agenda One

The "Learning Partners" module is an introduction exercise that helps to create the learning environment by preparing participants to act as learning partners with each other. The "What Is Coaching?" module sets the foundation for the rest of the coaching training, and the "Coaching Self-Assessment" module helps participants recognize learning opportunities that offer the greatest leverage for improving their coaching skills. The "Needs Assessment and Defining the Coaching Relationship" module helps them identify the needs of the people they are coaching and set clear expectations regarding the outcomes of the coaching process. Even with short breaks, this design extends past the four-hour mark.

 **TIME**

- ◆ 4 hours, 40 minutes

## MATERIALS

*For the instructor:*

- Content Module 10–1: Learning Partners

- Content Module 10–2: What Is Coaching?

- Content Module 10–3: Coaching Self-Assessment

- Content Module 10–4: Needs Assessment and Defining the Coaching Relationship

- Structured Experience 12–1: What Is Coaching?

- Structured Experience 12–2: I Want to Drive

- PowerPoint presentation: What Is Coaching. To access slides for this program, open the file *What Is Coaching.ppt* on the accompanying CD. Copies of the slides for this training session are included at the end of chapter 9 (slides 9–1 through 9–10).

- PowerPoint presentation: Assessing Coaching Needs. To access slides for this program, open the file *Assessing Coaching Needs.ppt* on the accompanying CD. Copies of the slides for this training session are included at the end of chapter 9 (slides 9–11 through 9–31).

*For the participants:*

- Assessment 11–2: Coaching Self-Assessment

- Assessment 11–6: Coaching Needs Assessment

- Training Instrument 11–1: Coaching Agreements Worksheet

## SAMPLE AGENDA

8:00 a.m.  Content Module 10–1: Learning Partners (chapter 10, page 98) (30 minutes; varies by class size)

*Objective:* Prepare participants to help each other learn

8:30  Content Module 10–2: What Is Coaching? (chapter 10, page 99) (1 hour)

*Objective:* Understand what coaching is and the importance of properly defining the coaching role.

| | |
|---|---|
| 9:30 | Break (5 minutes) |
| 9:35 | Content Module 10–3: Coaching Self-Assessment (chapter 10, page 100) (1 hour) |

*Objective:* Identify each participant's highest value learning opportunities

| | |
|---|---|
| 10:35 | Break (5 minutes) |
| 10:40 | Content Module 10–4: Needs Assessment and Defining the Coaching Relationship (chapter 10, page 101) (2 hours) |

*Objective:* Understand how to identify the highest leverage coaching needs of the person being coached.

| | |
|---|---|
| 12:40 | Close (5 minutes) |

*Objective:* Reinforce learning points.

## Sample Agenda Two

Including breaks, this design extends slightly past the four-hour mark. The "Building Trust and Rapport" module explores the importance of defining the boundaries of trust in a relationship and looks at ways to build trust between the coach and person being coached. The "Listening for Understanding" module looks at the importance of listening in the coaching role and covers techniques for effective listening.

 *TIME*

◆ 4 hours, 15 minutes

### MATERIALS

*For the instructor:*

◆ Content Module 10–5: Building Trust and Rapport

◆ Content Module 10–6: Listening for Understanding

 ◆ Structured Experience 12–3: Building Rapport

◆ Structured Experience 12–4: Trust Walk

- Structured Experience 12–5: Draw It

- PowerPoint presentation: Building Trust and Rapport. To access slides for this program, open the file *Building Trust and Rapport.ppt* on the accompanying CD. Copies of the slides for this training session are included at the end of chapter 9 (slides 9–40 through 9–46).

- PowerPoint presentation: Listening for Understanding. To access slides for this program, open the file *Listening for Understanding.ppt* on the accompanying CD. Copies of the slides for this training session are included at the end of chapter 9 (slides 9–47 through 9–53).

*For the participants:*

- Assessment 11–7: Listening Self-Assessment

## SAMPLE AGENDA

8:00 a.m.   Content Module 10–5: Building Trust and Rapport (chapter 10, page 103) (2.25 hours)

*Objective:* Understand the nature of trust and learn ways to build trust between the coach and person being coached.

10:15   Break (15 minutes)

10:30   Content Module 10–6: Listening for Understanding (chapter 10, page 105) (1.75 hours)

*Objective:* Understand the importance of listening and how to listen effectively.

12:15   Close (5 minutes)

*Objective:* Reinforce learning points.

## Sample Agenda Three

This agenda covers the "Giving Effective Feedback" and "Coach as Mentor" modules.

## TIME

- 3 hours, 30 minutes

### *MATERIALS*

*For the instructor:*

- ◆ Content Module 10–7: Giving Effective Feedback

- ◆ Content Module 10–11: Coach as Mentor

- ◆ Structured Experience 12–6: Team Theater

- ◆ Structured Experience 12–12: Mentoring Discussion

- ◆ PowerPoint presentation: Effective Feedback. To access slides for this program, open the file *Effective Feedback.ppt* on the accompanying CD. Copies of the slides for this training session are included at the end of chapter 9 (slides 9–54 through 9–63).

- ◆ PowerPoint presentation: Coach as Mentor. To access slides for this program, open the file *Coach as Mentor.ppt* on the accompanying CD. Copies of the slides for this training session are included at the end of chapter 9 (slides 9–94 through 9–99).

*For the participants:*

- ◆ Training Instrument 11–2: Feedback Preparation Worksheet

### *SAMPLE AGENDA*

8:00 a.m.　　Content Module 10–7: Giving Effective Feedback (chapter 10, page 109) (2.25 hours)

　　　　　　*Objective:* Learn principles and techniques for providing effective feedback.

10:15　　　　Break (15 minutes)

10:30　　　　Content Module 10–11: Coach as Mentor (chapter 10, page 117) (1 hour)

　　　　　　*Objective:* Understand how to help the person they are coaching succeed in their organizational context.

11:30　　　　Close (5 minutes)

　　　　　　*Objective:* Reinforce learning points.

## Sample Agenda Four

This agenda contains a single module: "Coach as Teacher."

### *TIME*

- ◆   2 hours, 45 minutes

### *MATERIALS*

*For the instructor:*

- ◆   Content Module 10–10: Coach as Teacher

- ◆   Structured Experience 12–8: Break it Down

- ◆   Structured Experience 12–9: Origami Knowledge Transfer

- ◆   Prizes

- ◆   PowerPoint presentation: Coach as Teacher. To access slides for this program, open the file *Coach as Teacher.ppt* on the accompanying CD. Copies of the slides for this training session are included at the end of chapter 9 (slides 9–74 through 9–85).

*For the participants:*

- ◆   Training Instrument 11–3: Process Steps Worksheet

- ◆   Three square pieces of paper for each participant. For folding, 8.5 × 8.5 works well and is easily cut from an 8.5 × 11–inch piece of paper.

- ◆   Origami instructions (half should receive the instructions for the swan and half the instructions for the frog).

### *SAMPLE AGENDA*

8:00 a.m.   Begin Content Module 10–10: Coach as Teacher (chapter 10, page 115) (1.25 hours)

*Objective:* Understand how to transfer knowledge effectively to another person.

9:15   Break (15 minutes)

9:30   Continue Content Module 10–10: Coach as Teacher (1.25 hours)

10:45      Close (5 minutes)

*Objective:* Reinforce learning points.

## Sample Agenda Five

This agenda contains the remaining two modules: "Coach as Guide" and "Coach as Motivator."

### TIME

- ◆ 3 hours, 15 minutes

### MATERIALS

*For the instructor:*

- ◆ Content Module 10–8: Coach as Guide

- ◆ Content Module 10–9: Coach as Motivator

- ◆ Structured Experience 12–7: Where Do I Want to Go?

- ◆ Structured Experience 12–11: What's Important to Me?

- ◆ PowerPoint presentation: Coach as Guide. To access slides for this program, open the file *Coach as Guide.ppt* on the accompanying CD. Copies of the slides for this training session are included at the end of chapter 9 (slides 9–64 through 9–73).

- ◆ PowerPoint presentation: Coach as Motivator. To access slides for this program, open the file *Coach as Motivator.ppt* on the accompanying CD. Copies of the slides for this training session are included at the end of chapter 9 (slides 9–86 through 9–93).

*For the participants:*

- ◆ Training Instrument 11–4: Values Worksheet

- ◆ Paper and writing materials

### SAMPLE AGENDA

8:00 a.m.     Content Module 10–8: Coach as Guide (chapter 10, page 111) (1.5 hours)

*Objective:* Understand how to help the person being coached create a vision and goals and evaluate progress.

9:30        Break (15 minutes)

9:45        Content Module 10–9: Coach as Motivator (chapter 10, page 113) (1.5 hours)

*Objective:* Understand how appropriate levels of confidence and reinforcing consequences can improve performance.

11:15       Close (5 minutes)

*Objective:* Reinforce learning points.

## Step-by-Step Planning

*Just prior to the training session:*

◆ Arrive early at the facility.

◆ Set up and test equipment (projectors, flipcharts, and so on).

◆ Confirm refreshments.

*At the first training session of the series:*

◆ Introduce yourself to the participants. Include a description of your role in the training process and your training and work experience. First impressions count, and this is your chance to establish credibility with the participants.

◆ If you do not run the learning partners exercise, ask the participants to introduce themselves. They should include their names, roles, and coaching experiences. Let them know they will be helping each other learn.

◆ Review the agenda and learning objectives with the participants.

◆ Go through the selected content module(s).

◆ Ask for questions and test for understanding frequently.

◆ Close the session with an opportunity for the participants to ask questions. If appropriate, offer your help and availability on an ongoing basis.

*At the second through fifth sessions:*

- ◆ Review the agenda and learning objectives with the participants.

- ◆ Go through the selected content module(s).

- ◆ Ask for questions and test for understanding frequently.

- ◆ Close the session with an opportunity for the participants to ask questions. If appropriate, offer your help and availability on an ongoing basis.

## What to Do Next

- ◆ Identify the training participants and assess their most critical training needs or identify the competencies the organization seeks to develop.

- ◆ Design the agenda based on the highest value content modules called for by needs or required competencies identified.

- ◆ Schedule the session.

- ◆ Arrange a facility for the training session.

- ◆ Invite participants.

- ◆ Send a confirmation to participants. Include an agenda and any pre-work with the confirmation.

- ◆ Prepare training materials (handouts, overheads, presentations, teamwork exercise materials).

- ◆ Order food and drinks.

# Chapter 8

# Full-Day Session

**What's in This Chapter?**

- ◆ Advice on choosing the content for training sessions
- ◆ Step-by-step preparation and training delivery instructions
- ◆ Sample agendas

The workbook materials have been designed to meet a variety of training needs and timeframes. This chapter covers designs suitable for full-day (six- to eight-hour) training sessions.

Full-day (and longer) learning experiences might raise concerns that participants will be overloaded with information. However, the benefits of extended learning experiences can outweigh the potential drawbacks. Although a shorter program might be seen as part of a typical workday, a longer program (particularly if held at an offsite venue) can become a memorable life experience for the participant. The learning environment discussed in chapter 4 is more readily established in extended programs in which the synergistic relationships of the various coaching competencies can be more thoroughly explored. It often takes a different physical environment and a complete break from daily routine for participants to focus on learning.

Full-day sessions are appropriate for group training. The learning environment is enhanced by the backgrounds and experiences of a variety of participants. For full-day sessions, groups of between 12 and 24 participants are most conducive to a learning environment.

Although this chapter includes illustrative designs, the trainer should adapt them to fit the training purposes. Each design can be modified to take into account the resources available, the learning readiness of potential participants, and—above all—the assessed development needs of the coaches and the organization.

## Objectives and Use

The objectives of a full-day training session are to free participants from their daily routine so they are open to develop an understanding of the learning content that is of greatest value and to build relationships between the trainer and the participants. The group setting and time available for interaction allow for rich and diverse discussion of the various topics.

A full-day training session is appropriate for the following circumstances:

- ◆ The targeted, available audience for training is 12 or more.

- ◆ The targeted audience requires training in several areas of content.

- ◆ Training facilities for groups are available.

- ◆ A full day is available for the training session.

- ◆ Funding for meals and (optionally) for an offsite location is available.

## Choosing the Content

Any of the content modules in this book can be used as part of a full-day training session. Select the modules based on the needs assessment of the participant group. If the participant group does not have an identified set of assessed needs (an assessment was not completed or an open registration process is being used), select the modules based on the competencies the organization seeks to develop.

As noted for the half-day sessions, the entire curriculum contained in this workbook also can be offered in a series of full-day sessions.

 When your training session is at least a full day long, you've crossed over the meal threshold. Hunger and thirst are enemies to the learning environment. Offer drinks and snacks at the breaks so your participants' biological needs are met. Lunch for participants is strongly suggested. Keeping participants together during the lunch break encourages continuing discussion of learning points. It also helps to strengthen the relationships between participants and, therefore, helps support the learning environment. In addition, a scheduled lunch discourages participants from going "back to the office" and getting

distracted from their learning focus. Finally, providing lunch helps to keep your class on schedule as participants are less likely to come back late from the lunch break.

Three sample agendas are included. Each is designed as a standalone training session. Each agenda reflects a different major training issue pertaining to coaching.

## Sample Agenda One

This agenda reflects a requirement for training on the coaching competency of transferring knowledge. This requirement could have been identified as an organizational competency or as a common need for the participants. The timing of the module "Coach as Teacher" assumes that the large-group structured experience "Snowflake" is included.

### TIME

- ◆ 8 hours, 15 minutes

### MATERIALS

*For the instructor:*

- ◆ Content Module 10–1: Learning Partners

- ◆ Content Module 10–2: What Is Coaching?

- ◆ Content Module 10–6: Listening for Understanding

- ◆ Content Module 10–10: Coach as Teacher

- ◆ Structured Experience 12–1: What Is Coaching?

- ◆ Structured Experience 12–5: Draw It

- ◆ Structured Experience 12–8: Break It Down

- ◆ Structured Experience 12–9: Origami Knowledge Transfer

- ◆ Structured Experience 12–10: Snowflake

- ◆ Prizes

- ◆ PowerPoint presentation: What Is Coaching? To access slides for this program, open the file *What Is Coaching.ppt* on the accompanying

CD. Copies of the slides for this training session are included at the end of chapter 9 (slides 9–1 through 9–10).

◆ PowerPoint presentation: Listening for Understanding. To access slides for this program, open the file *Listening for Understanding.ppt* on the accompanying CD. Copies of the slides for this training session are included at the end of chapter 9 (slides 9–47 through 9–53).

◆ PowerPoint presentation: Coach as Teacher. To access slides for this program, open the file *Coach as Teacher.ppt* on the accompanying CD. Copies of the slides for this training session are included at the end of chapter 9 (slides 9–74 through 9–85).

*For the participants:*

◆ Assessment 11–7: Listening Self-Assessment

◆ Training Instrument 11–3: Process Steps Worksheet

◆ Origami exercise instructions (half should receive the instructions for the swan and half the instructions for the frog)

◆ Three 8.5 × 8.5–inch pieces of paper for each participant for the Origami exercise.

◆ Writing instruments and paper

◆ One copy of diagrams 1 and 2 from Structured Experience 12–5: "Draw It" for each pair of participants

◆ Paper for the "Snowflake" structured experience

◆ Scissors

### SAMPLE AGENDA

8:00 a.m.  Content Module 10–1: Learning Partners (chapter 10, page 98) (45 minutes; varies by class size)

*Objective:* Prepare participants to help each other learn.

8:45  Content Module 10–2: What Is Coaching? (chapter 10, page 99) (1 hour)

*Objective:* Understand what coaching is and the importance of properly defining the coaching role.

9:45          Break (15 minutes)

10:00        Content Module 10–6: Listening for Understanding (chapter 10, page 105) (1.75 hours)

               *Objective:* Understand the importance of listening and how to listen effectively.

11:45        Lunch (1 hour)

12:45 p.m.  Content Module 10–10: Coach as Teacher (chapter 10, page 115) (3.5 hours)

               *Objective:* Understand how to transfer knowledge effectively to another person.

4:15          Close

## Sample Agenda Two

This agenda is based on an identified need to improve the ability of coaches to guide and motivate others.

### TIME

◆ 8 hours, 30 minutes

### MATERIALS

*For the instructor:*

◆ Content Module 10–1: Learning Partners

◆ Content Module 10–2: What Is Coaching?

◆ Content Module 10–7: Giving Effective Feedback

◆ Content Module 10–8: Coach as Guide

◆ Content Module 10–9: Coach as Motivator

◆ Structured Experience 12–1: What Is Coaching?

◆ Structured Experience 12–6: Team Theater

◆ Structured Experience 12–7: Where Do I Want to Go?

◆ Structured Experience 12–11: What's Important to Me?

◆ PowerPoint presentation: What Is Coaching. To access slides for this program, open the file *What Is Coaching.ppt* on the accompanying CD. Copies of the slides for this training session are included at the end of chapter 9 (slides 9–1 through 9–10).

◆ PowerPoint presentation: Effective Feedback. To access slides for this program, open the file *Effective Feedback.ppt* on the accompanying CD. Copies of the slides for this training session are included at the end of chapter 9 (slides 9–54 through 9–63).

◆ PowerPoint presentation: Coach as Guide. To access slides for this program, open the file *Coach as Guide.ppt* on the accompanying CD. Copies of the slides for this training session are included at the end of chapter 9 (slides 9–64 through 9–73).

◆ PowerPoint presentation: Coach as Motivator. To access slides for this program, open the file *Coach as Motivator.ppt* on the accompanying CD. Copies of the slides for this training session are included at the end of chapter 9 (slides 9–86 through 9–93).

*For the participants:*

◆ Training Instrument 11–2: Feedback Preparation Worksheet

◆ Training Instrument 11–4: Values Worksheet

### SAMPLE AGENDA

8:00 a.m.    Content Module 10–1: Learning Partners (chapter 10, page 98) (45 minutes; varies by class size)

*Objective:* Prepare participants to help each other learn.

8:45    Content Module 10–2: What Is Coaching? (chapter 10, page 99) (1 hour)

*Objective:* Understand what coaching is and the importance of properly defining the coaching role.

9:45    Break (15 minutes)

10:00    Content Module 10–7: Giving Effective Feedback (chapter 10, page 109) (2.25 hours)

*Objective:* Learn principles and techniques for providing effective feedback.

12:15 p.m.  Lunch (1 hour)

1:15  Content Module 10–9: Coach as Motivator (chapter 10, page 113) (1.5 hours)

*Objective:* Understand how appropriate levels of confidence and reinforcing consequences can improve performance.

2:45  Break (15 minutes)

3:00  Content Module 10–8: Coach as Guide (chapter 10, page 111) (1.5 hours)

*Objective:* Understand how to help the person being coached create a vision and goals and evaluate progress.

4:30  Close

## Sample Agenda Three

This agenda is designed to strengthen the mentoring skills of the participants.

### *TIME*

  ◆  7 hours, 30 minutes

### *MATERIALS*

*For the instructor:*

  ◆  Content Module 10–1: Learning Partners

  ◆  Content Module 10–5: Building Trust and Rapport

  ◆  Content Module 10–7: Giving Effective Feedback

  ◆  Content Module 10–11: Coach as Mentor

  ◆  Structured Experience 12–3: Building Rapport

  ◆  Structured Experience 12–4: Trust Walk

  ◆  Structured Experience 12–6: Team Theater

  ◆  Structured Experience 12–12: Mentoring Discussion

◆ PowerPoint presentation: Building Trust and Rapport. To access slides for this program, open the file *Building Trust and Rapport.ppt* on the accompanying CD. Copies of the slides for this training session are included at the end of this chapter 9 (slides 9–40 through 9–46).

◆ PowerPoint presentation: Effective Feedback. To access slides for this program, open the file *Effective Feedback.ppt* on the accompanying CD. Copies of the slides for this training session are included at the end of this chapter 9 (slides 9–54 through 9–63).

◆ PowerPoint presentation: Coach as Mentor. To access slides for this program, open the file *Coach as Mentor.ppt* on the accompanying CD. Copies of the slides for this training session are included at the end of this chapter 9 (slides 9–94 through 9–99).

*For the participants:*

◆ Training Instrument 11–2: Feedback Preparation Worksheet

◆ Blindfolds for each participant

## SAMPLE AGENDA

9:00 a.m.    Content Module 10–1: Learning Partners module (chapter 10, page 98) (45 minutes; varies by class size)

*Objective:* Prepare participants to help each other learn.

9:45    Content Module 10–5: Building Trust and Rapport (chapter 10, page 103) (2.25 hours)

*Objective:* Understand the nature of trust and learn ways to build trust between the coach and person being coached.

Noon    Lunch (1 hour)

1:00 p.m.    Content Module 10–11: Coach as Mentor (chapter 10, page 117) (1 hour)

*Objective:* Understand how to help the person being coached succeed in his or her organizational context.

2:00    Break (15 minutes)

2:15       Content Module 10–7: Giving Effective Feedback (chapter 10, page 109) (2.25 hours)

*Objective:* Learn principles and techniques for providing effective feedback.

4:30       Close

*Objective:* Reinforce learning points.

## Step-by-Step Planning

*Just before the training session:*

- Arrive early at the facility.

- Set up and test equipment (projectors, flipcharts, and so forth).

- Confirm food and drinks.

*At each training session:*

- Introduce yourself to the participants. Include a description of your role in the training process and your training and work experience. First impressions count, and this is your chance to establish credibility with the participants.

- If you do not run the learning partners exercise, ask the participants to introduce themselves. They should include their names, roles, and coaching experiences. Let them know that they will be helping each other learn.

- Review the agenda and learning objectives with the participants.

- Go through the selected content module(s).

- Ask for questions and test for understanding frequently.

- Close the session with an opportunity for the participants to ask questions. If appropriate, offer your help and availability on an ongoing basis.

## What to Do Next

♦ Identify the training participants and assess their most critical training needs or identify the competencies the organization seeks to develop.

♦ Design the agenda based on the highest value content modules based on the needs identification.

♦ Schedule the session.

♦ Arrange a facility for the training session.

♦ Invite participants. Check for any special dietary needs.

♦ Send a confirmation to participants. Include an agenda and any pre-work with the confirmation.

♦ Prepare training materials (handouts, overheads, presentations, teamwork exercise materials).

♦ Order food and drinks.

# Chapter 9

# Multi-Day Session

**What's in This Chapter?**

- ◆ Advice on choosing the content for training sessions
- ◆ Step-by-step preparation and training delivery instructions
- ◆ Sample agendas

The materials in this workbook have been designed to meet a variety of training needs and timeframes. This chapter covers a design suitable for a multi-day training session.

As noted in chapter 8, longer learning experiences might raise concerns that participants will be overloaded with information. You can avoid the overload issue by designing programs that allow participants to learn efficiently and at their own pace. The purpose of this chapter is to present a significant amount of content in a multi-day session by mixing short, to-the-point theory and models with experiential exercises and assessments. This keeps the participants from feeling like they are "drinking from a fire hose" and, instead, produces an enjoyable, fruitful leaning experience. In addition, there are important benefits associated with extended learning experiences. Although a shorter program might be seen as part of a typical workday, a longer program (particularly if held at an offsite venue and including an overnight stay) can become a memorable life experience for the participant. A multi-day design provides ample opportunity to create the learning environment (chapter 4) and establish participants as learning partners. Discussion during breaks, meals, and evening activities often provides valuable feedback and learning. Also, it often takes a different physical environment and a complete break from daily routine for participants to focus on learning.

Multi-day sessions are appropriate for group training. The learning environment is created and enriched by the backgrounds and experiences of a variety of participants. For multi-day sessions, groups of 12 to 24 participants are most conducive to a learning environment. Smaller groups can limit the richness of group interactions and larger groups can become unwieldy for the facilitator and can depersonalize the learning experience.

Please note that, although illustrative designs are included, the trainer should adapt them to fit his or her specific purposes. Each design can be modified to take into account the resources available, the learning readiness of potential participants, and—above all—the assessed development needs of the target audience.

## Objectives and Use

The objectives of a multi-day training session are to free participants from their daily routines so they are open to develop an understanding of the learning content that is of greatest value and to build relationships among the trainer and the participants. The group setting and time available for interaction allows for rich and diverse discussion of the various topics.

*Note:* Residential programs held at appealing facilities also can be used to reward participants for the responsibilities they assume when they take on coaching assignments.

A multi-day training session is appropriate for the following circumstances:

◆ The targeted, available audience for training is 12 or more.

◆ The targeted audience requires comprehensive training in all areas of relevant content.

◆ Training facilities for groups are available.

◆ Participants are available for multiple days.

◆ Funding for meals and (optionally) for an offsite location is available.

## Choosing the Content

Any of the content modules in this book can be used for multi-day training sessions. Although a multi-day session allows time to cover all the content modules, you may still need to perform a needs assessment of the participant

Multi-Day Session ♦ 69

group or review the competencies the organization seeks to develop. Include only those modules indicated by your needs assessment.

With a session that covers multiple days, you've crossed over the meal and, possibly, the overnight thresholds. Hunger and thirst are enemies of the learning environment. Offer drinks and snacks at the breaks, as well as meals, so your participants' biological needs are met. Keeping participants together during meals encourages continuation of discussion of learning points. It also helps strengthen the relationships between participants and, therefore, helps support the learning environment. Much discussion and feedback occurs during dinner after a long day of training. As noted in chapter 8, scheduled meals discourage participants from going back to the office and getting distracted from their learning focus. Also, providing meals helps to keep your class on schedule as participants are less likely to come back late from the lunch break.

The following sample agenda covers all of the content modules in this book in a three-day session. The timing of the "Coach as Teacher" module assumes that the large-group structured experience "Snowflake" is included.

The placement of the "Learning Partners," "What Is Coaching?" and "Coaching Self-Assessment" modules in the program is important. They should be offered at the beginning of the session because they help focus the learning of participants by creating the context for the remaining content modules.

## Sample Agenda (Day One)

### *MATERIALS*

*For the instructor:*

- ♦ Content Module 10–1: Learning Partners

- ♦ Content Module 10–2: What Is Coaching?

- ♦ Content Module 10–3: Coaching Self-Assessment

- ♦ Content Module 10–4: Needs Assessment and Defining the Coaching Relationship

- ♦ Content Module 10–5: Building Trust and Rapport

- ♦ Structured Experience 12–1: What Is Coaching?

- ♦ Structured Experience 12–3: Building Rapport

◆ Structured Experience 12–4: Trust Walk

◆ PowerPoint presentation: Building Trust and Rapport. To access slides for this program, open the file *Building Trust and Rapport.ppt* on the accompanying CD. Copies of the slides for this training session are included at the end of this chapter (slides 9–40 through 9–46).

◆ PowerPoint presentation: What Is Coaching? To access slides for this program, open the file *What Is Coaching.ppt* on the accompanying CD. Copies of the slides for this training session are included at the end of this chapter (slides 9–1 through 9–10).

◆ PowerPoint presentation: Coaching Needs Assessment. To access slides for this program, open the file *Assessing Coaching Needs.ppt* on the accompanying CD. Copies of the slides for this training session are included at the end of this chapter (slides 9–11 through 9–31).

◆ PowerPoint presentation: Defining the Coaching Relationship. To access slides for this program, open the file *Defining the Coaching Relationship.ppt* on the accompanying CD. Copies of the slides for this training session are included at the end of this chapter (slides 9–32 through 9–39).

*For the participants:*

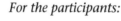

◆ Assessment 11–2: Coaching Self-Assessment

◆ Assessment 11–6: Coaching Needs Assessment

### SAMPLE AGENDA

8:00 a.m.    Content Module 10–1: Learning Partners (chapter 10, page 98) (45 minutes; varies by class size)

*Objective:* Prepare participants to help each other learn.

8:45    Content Module 10–2: What Is Coaching? (chapter 10, page 99) (1 hour)

*Objective:* Understand what coaching is and the importance of properly defining the coaching role.

9:45    Break (15 minutes)

10:00    Content Module 10–3: Coaching Self-Assessment (chapter 10, page 100) (1 hour)

*Objective:* Identify each participant's highest value learning opportunities.

11:00     Begin Content Module 10–4: Needs Assessment and Defining the Coaching Relationship (chapter 10, page 101) (1 hour)

*Objective:* Understand how to identify the highest leverage coaching needs of the person being coached.

Noon     Lunch (1 hour)

1:00 p.m.     Complete Content Module 10–4: Needs Assessment and Defining the Coaching Relationship (1 hour)

2:00     Break (15 minutes)

2:15     Content Module 10–5: Building Trust and Rapport (chapter 10, page 103) (2.25 hours)

*Objective:* Understand the nature of trust and learn ways to build trust between the coach and person being coached.

4:30     Close

6:00     Dinner (if at an offsite location)

7:00     After-dinner activities (if at a residential offsite location)

## Sample Agenda (Day Two)

### MATERIALS

*For the instructor:*

- ◆ Content Module 10–6: Listening for Understanding

- ◆ Content Module 10–7: Giving Effective Feedback

- ◆ Content Module 10–8: Coach as Guide

- ◆ Content Module 10–9: Coach as Motivator

- ◆ Structured Experience 12–6: Team Theater

- ◆ Structured Experience 12–7: Where Do I Want to Go?

- ◆ Structured Experience 12–11: What's Important to Me?

◆ PowerPoint presentation: Listening for Understanding. To access slides for this program, open the file *Listening for Understanding.ppt* on the accompanying CD. Copies of the slides for this training session are included at the end of this chapter (slides 9–47 through 9–53).

◆ PowerPoint presentation: Effective Feedback. To access slides for this program, open the file *Effective Feedback.ppt* on the accompanying CD. Copies of the slides for this training session are included at the end of this chapter (slides 9–54 through 9–63).

◆ PowerPoint presentation: Coach as Guide. To access slides for this program, open the file *Coach as Guide.ppt* on the accompanying CD. Copies of the slides for this training session are included at the end of this chapter (slides 9–64 through 9–73).

◆ PowerPoint presentation: Coach as Motivator. To access slides for this program, open the file *Coach as Motivator.ppt* on the accompanying CD. Copies of the slides for this training session are included at the end of this chapter (slides 9–86 through 9–93).

*For the participants:*

◆ Training Instrument 11–2: Feedback Preparation Worksheet

◆ Training Instrument 11–4: Values Worksheet

◆ Paper and writing materials

## SAMPLE AGENDA

8:00 a.m.   Open and Review

*Objective:* Reset learning environment; present agenda.

8:10   Content Module 10–6: Listening for Understanding (chapter 10, page 105) (1.75 hours)

*Objective:* Understand the importance of listening and how to listen effectively.

9:55   Break (15 minutes)

10:10   Content Module 10–7: Giving Effective Feedback (chapter 10, page 109) (2.25 hours)

*Objective:* Learn principles and techniques for providing effective feedback.

12:25 p.m.   Lunch (65 minutes)

1:30   Content Module 10–8: Coach as Guide (chapter 10, page 111) (1.5 hours)

*Objective:* Understand how to help the person being coached create a vision and goals and evaluate progress.

3:00   Break (15 minutes)

3:15   Content Module 10–9: Coach as Motivator (chapter 10, page 113) (1.5 hours)

*Objective:* Understand how appropriate levels of confidence and reinforcing consequences can improve performance.

4:45   Close

*Objective:* Reinforce learning point

6:00   Dinner (if at an offsite location)

7:00   After-dinner activities (if at a residential offsite location)

# Sample Agenda (Day Three)

## MATERIALS

*For the instructor:*

- Content Module 10–10: Coach as Teacher

- Content Module 10–11: Coach as Mentor

- Structured Experience 12–8: Break It Down

- Structured Experience 12–9: Origami Knowledge Transfer

- Structured Experience 12–10: Snowflake

- Structured Experience 12–12: Mentoring Discussion

- PowerPoint presentation: Coach as Teacher. To access slides for this program, open the file *Coach as Teacher.ppt* on the accompanying

CD. Copies of the slides for this training session are included at the end of this chapter (slides 9–74 through 9–85).

◆ PowerPoint presentation: Coach as Mentor. To access slides for this program, open the file *Coach as Mentor.ppt* on the accompanying CD. Copies of the slides for this training session are included at the end of this chapter (slides 9–94 through 9–99).

◆ Prizes

*For the participants:*

◆ Training Instrument 11–3: Process Steps Worksheet

◆ Origami instructions (half should receive the instructions for the swan and half the instructions for the frog)

◆ Three 8.5 × 8.5–inch pieces of paper for each participant for the "Origami" exercise

◆ Paper for the "Snowflake" exercise

◆ Scissors

## SAMPLE AGENDA

9:00 a.m.   Begin Content Module 10–10: Coach as Teacher (chapter 10, page 115) (.25 hour)

*Objective:* Understand how to transfer knowledge effectively to another person.

9:15   Break (15 minutes)

9:30   Continue Content Module 10–10: Coach as Teacher (1.25 hours)

10:45   Break (15 minutes)

11:00   Continue Coach as Teacher (1 hour)

Noon   Lunch (1 hour)

1:00 p.m.   Content Module 10–11: Coach as Mentor (chapter 10, page 117) (1 hour)

*Objective:* Understand how to help the person being coached succeed in his or her organizational context.

2:00　　　　Close

*Objective:* Reinforce learning points.

## Step-by-Step Planning

*Just before the training session:*

- ◆ If this is a residential program, confirm rooming list with hotel.

- ◆ Arrive early at the facility.

- ◆ Set up and test equipment (projectors, flipcharts, and so forth).

- ◆ Confirm food and drinks.

*At the training session:*

- ◆ Introduce yourself to the participants. Include a description of your role in the training process and your training and work experience. First impressions count, and this is your chance to establish credibility with the participants.

- ◆ If you do not run the learning partners exercise, ask the participants to introduce themselves. They should include their names, roles, and coaching experiences. Let them know that they will be helping each other learn.

- ◆ Review each day's agenda and learning objectives with the participants.

- ◆ Go through the selected content module(s).

- ◆ Ask for questions and test for understanding frequently.

- ◆ Close each day with an opportunity for the participants to ask questions.

## What to Do Next

- ◆ Identify the training participants and assess their most critical training needs or identify the competencies the organization seeks to develop.

- ◆ Design the agenda based on the highest value content modules to address the needs or the required competencies identified.

- ◆  Schedule the session.

- ◆  Arrange a facility for the training session. Book a block of rooms if this is a residential program.

- ◆  Invite participants. Check for any special dietary needs. If this is a residential program, check for rooming requirements (smoking/non-smoking, single/double bed, and so forth).

- ◆  Send a confirmation to participants. Include an agenda and any pre-work with the confirmation.

- ◆  Prepare training materials (handouts, overheads, presentations, teamwork exercise materials).

- ◆  Order food and drinks.

**Slide 9–1**

# What Is Coaching?

Chris Chen

American Society for Training & Development

9-1

**Slide 9–2**

## Coaching Is...

- In general, coaching is helping someone else expand and apply his or her skills, knowledge, and abilities.
- For this program, coaching is defined as helping others succeed through guiding, teaching, motivating, and mentoring.

9-2

**Slide 9–3**

## Coach as Guide

- Defining "success"
- Creating a vision of the future
- Setting goals
- Action planning
- Evaluating progress

9-3

**Slide 9–4**

## Coach as Teacher

- Transferring knowledge or skills to the person you are coaching

9-4

**Slide 9–5**

## Coach as Motivator

- Helping the person you are coaching find meaning in his or her role/task/assignment
- Building confidence
- Identifying reinforcing consequences

9-5

**Slide 9–6**

## Coach as Mentor

- Enabling the person you are coaching to effectively use his or her personal traits and skills in the context of organizational realities

9-6

**Slide 9–7**

## Defining a Specific Context

- Who?
- What?
  - Task
  - Skill
  - Responsibility
- How long?
- What are the expected outcomes?

9-7

**Slide 9–8**

## Good Coaching...

- Transfers knowledge on a "just-in-time" basis.
- Disperses expertise throughout an organization.
- Increases individual motivation and morale.
- Helps individuals and organizations achieve outstanding results.
- Have you ever had a good coach? What was it like?

9-8

**Slide 9–9**

## Bad Coaching...

- Wastes the time of valuable resources.
- Creates a hostile work environment.
- Creates suboptimal organizations and ineffective individuals.
- Have you ever had a bad coach? What was it like?

9-9

**Slide 9–10**

## For a Successful Coaching Engagement...

- Clearly define the scope and expected results of the coaching engagement.
- Align expectations between the coach and the person being coached.

9-10

**Slide 9–11**

## Assessing Coaching Needs

American Society for Training & Development

9-11

**Slide 9–12**

## Four Roles of Coaches

- Coach as Guide
- Coach as Teacher
- Coach as Motivator
- Coach as Mentor

9-12

*Slide 9–13*

## Coach as Guide
## Assessment Items

Does the person you are coaching…

- Have a clear understanding of his or her role in the organization?
- Have clearly defined tasks/responsibilities?
- Have a clear understanding of what it means to be successful regarding those tasks/responsibilities?
- Have a plan to accomplish the task or fulfill the responsibility?

9-13

*Slide 9–14*

## Coach as Guide

- Have a clear understanding of his or her role in the organization?
  - Does the person understand what the organization is trying to accomplish and how his or her skills and abilities can contribute?
  - Finding/defining the appropriate fit in the organization is the first step to success.

9-14

*Slide 9–15*

## Coach as Guide

- Have clearly defined tasks/responsibilities?
  - Can the person articulate the specific tasks and responsibilities that compose his or her role?
  - Help to create discrete, specific definitions of tasks and responsibilities so the person can focus on issues important to success.

9-15

*Slide 9–16*

## Coach as Guide

- Have a clear understanding of what it means to be successful regarding those tasks/responsibilities?
  - Does the person know how his or her achievements will be measured?
  - Ensure common understanding of the evaluation process and the metrics of results between the person being coached and the supervisor.

9-16

*Slide 9–17*

## Coach as Guide

- Have a plan to accomplish the task or fulfill the responsibility?
  - Has the person identified achievable, interim steps that, when accomplished in sequence, will result in successful completion of tasks?
  - Help him or her construct a plan with milestones, interim measures, required resources, and possible obstacles.

9-17

*Slide 9–18*

## Coach as Teacher
## Assessment Items

Does the person you are coaching…

- Possess the skills to accomplish/fulfill the task/responsibility?
- Possess the knowledge necessary to accomplish/fulfill the task/responsibility?

9-18

## Slide 9–19

### Coach as Teacher

- Possess the skills to accomplish/fulfill the task/responsibility?
  - Can the person acquire the skills needed?
  - Does he or she possess required natural abilities?
  - Why doesn't he or she have the required skills?
  - Is it really an issue of lack of skill or is it lack of motivation?
  - Responsibility for learning resides with the learner.

9-19

## Slide 9–20

### Coach as Teacher

- Possess the knowledge necessary to accomplish/fulfill the task/responsibility?
  - Does the person know what he or she doesn't know?
  - Help the person distinguish between the important and the less relevant.

9-20

## Slide 9–21

### Coach as Motivator
### Assessment Items

Does the person you are coaching…

- Have a high level of commitment to the task/responsibility?
- Have an awareness of positive consequences that will result from success and negative consequences that will result from failure?
- Have a firm belief that he or she can accomplish/handle the task/responsibility?
- Find the task/responsibility interesting and/or enjoyable?
- Have a natural inclination/aversion to the task/responsibility?

9-21

## Slide 9–22

### Coach as Motivator

- Have a high level of commitment to the task/responsibility?
  - Does the person feel a sense of ownership for completion of the task?
  - Does the person believe the task is important?

9-22

## Slide 9–23

### Coach as Motivator

- Have an awareness of positive consequences that will result from success and negative consequences that will result from failure?
  - Are there consequences directly tied to his or her performance?
  - Does the coach control or influence any of the consequences?
  - What value does the person place on those consequences?

9-23

## Slide 9–24

### Coach as Motivator

- Have a firm belief he or she can accomplish/handle the task/responsibility?
  - Is the person under- or overconfident?
  - Is his or her level of confidence based on actual experience?
  - Is this level of confidence rational?

9-24

**Slide 9–25**

## Coach as Motivator

- Find the task/responsibility interesting and/or enjoyable?
  - Is the person appropriately challenged by his or her responsibilities?
  - Does the person have fun in his or her role?
  - Does the person find meaning in his or her role?

9-25

**Slide 9–26**

## Coach as Motivator

- Have a natural inclination/aversion to the task/responsibility?
  - Does his or her role seem to fit his or her personality?
  - Did the person choose his or her role or did circumstances place him or her there?
  - Does the person have other role options or could he or she develop options?

9-26

**Slide 9–27**

## Coach as Mentor
## Assessment Items

Does the person you are coaching...
- Have a clear understanding of his or her role in the organization?
- Have clearly defined tasks/responsibilities?
- Have a well-defined career path?
- Understand his or her career interests?
- Have a good understanding of the culture and norms of the organization he or she is in?

9-27

**Slide 9–28**

## Coach as Mentor

- Have a clear understanding of his or her role in the organization?
- Have clearly defined tasks/responsibilities?
  - These items overlap with the "guide" role.
  - The person is critical to succeeding in the context of the organization.

9-28

**Slide 9–29**

## Coach as Mentor

- Have a well-defined career path?
  - What's the next step in the person's career?
  - Does the person know what kind of position he or she would like to have in the future?
  - How does the person's current position advance him or her toward future goals?

9-29

**Slide 9–30**

## Coach as Mentor

- Understand his or her career interests?
  - What role does career play in his or her life?
  - What is his or her ultimate career goal?
  - What would his or her dream job be?

9-30

**Slide 9–31**

## Coach as Mentor

- Have a good understanding of the culture and norms of his or her organization?
  - Does he or she know how things get done in the organization?
  - Does he or she know how decisions are made?
  - Is he or she well connected in the organization?
  - Does he or she feel comfortable and "at home" in the organization?

9-31

**Slide 9–32**

## Defining the Coaching Relationship

American Society for Training & Development

9-32

**Slide 9–33**

## The Coaching Contract...

- Aligns expectations between coach and the person being coached.
- Engages the person being coached in the coaching process.
- Keeps the coaching process manageable for the coach.

9-33

**Slide 9–34**

## S.C.O.R.E.

- Scope
- Consequences
- Outcomes
- Roles
- Evaluation

9-34

**Slide 9–35**

## Scope

- Who is being coached?
- What is the coach coaching on?
- How long will the coaching relationship exist?

9-35

**Slide 9–36**

## Consequences

- What are the consequences of success or failure for the coach and the person being coached?
- Who controls those consequences?

9-36

*Slide 9–37*

## Outcomes

- What are the desired outcomes of the coaching engagement?
- How does the coach define "success"?
- How does the person being coached define "success"?

9-37

*Slide 9–38*

## Roles

- What is the coach's responsibility?
- What is the responsibility of the person being coached?
- Are there any other stakeholders in the coaching process?
- What are the responsibilities of those stakeholders?

9-38

*Slide 9–39*

## Evaluation

- Will the results of the coaching engagement be measured?
- How will success or failure be measured?
- Who will do the measurement?
- Will the coach be evaluated?

9-39

*Slide 9–40*

## Building Trust and Rapport

American Society for Training & Development

9-40

*Slide 9–41*

## Two Aspects of Trust

- Trust in another's <u>motivation</u>
  - Do their intentions align with yours?
- Trust in another's <u>competence</u>
  - Do they have the ability to carry out those intentions?

9-41

*Slide 9–42*

## Context of Trust

- Trust is most easily established when the boundaries of that trust are clearly defined.
  - Who?
  - Regarding what responsibility?
  - For how long?
- Trust helps build healthy relationships when the trustor and trustee share a common understanding of the boundaries.

9-42

**Slide 9–43**

## Discussion Question

- What are some ways to build trust in a relationship?

9-43

**Slide 9–44**

## Building Trust

- Trust begets trust
  - If you show trust in someone else, he or she is more likely to trust you in return.
- Self-disclosure
  - Judiciously disclosing personal or private information demonstrates trust.
- Make eye contact
  - The eyes have been called the "windows to the soul."

9-44

**Slide 9–45**

## Building Trust

- Honor the other's skills and accomplishments
  - But push for change, if appropriate.
- Common self-interests
  - Most people trust others to pursue their own self-interests.
  - Build trust by showing how your self-interest aligns with the other person's self-interest.

9-45

**Slide 9–46**

## Building Rapport

- People are more alike than different.
- Relationships are strengthened when we focus on similarities
- Avoid the tendency to focus on disagreements.
- Key: Focus on something you respect in the other person.

9-46

**Slide 9–47**

## Listening for Understanding

American Society for Training & Development

9-47

**Slide 9–48**

## Keys to Effective Listening

- **Focus** – Paying complete attention to the speaker and the message he or she is trying to convey
- **Feedback** – Actively engaging the speaker through encouraging words and gestures, clarifying questions, and summarizing key points
- **Filtering** – Creating personal meaning from the speaker's comments; putting the speaker's comments in context with your own experiences, knowledge, and perceptions

9-48

*Slide 9–49*

## Focus

- Face the speaker.
- Make eye contact.
- Don't let your brain outrun the conversation.
- Pay attention to physical and verbal cues.
- Take your time in responding.

9-49

*Slide 9–50*

## Feedback

- Verbal
  - Ask clarifying questions.
  - Restate or paraphrase comments.
  - Use listening comments such as, "I see," "uh-huh," or "oh really."
  - Summarize facts, feelings conveyed, or other key points.
  - Don't interrupt the speaker to make listening comments, paraphrases, or summaries.

9-50

*Slide 9–51*

## Feedback

- Nonverbal
  - Face the speaker.
  - Maintain eye contact.
  - Adopt a listening posture.
  - Change your body posture if you find yourself drifting.
  - Keep arms at your side or hands in your lap.

9-51

*Slide 9–52*

## Filtering

- Concentrate on what the speaker is trying to say.
  - Don't mentally argue or judge comments prematurely.
- Avoid emotional reactions until the conversation is complete.
  - Try to remain objective and open-minded.
- Be judicious in anticipating statements.

9-52

*Slide 9–53*

## The Power of Silence

- Silence can be a powerful tool for eliciting information.
- Silence during a conversation is uncomfortable and people feel compelled to break it.
- Be silent, but engaged (maintain eye contact and listening posture) and the other person usually will volunteer more information on whatever topic is being addressed.

9-53

*Slide 9–54*

## Effective Feedback

American Society for Training & Development

9-54

**Slide 9–55**

## A Model for Giving Feedback

- Situation
- Behavior
- Impact

9-55

**Slide 9–56**

## Situation

- Start by identifying the situation.
- Where did the behavior take place?
- When did the behavior take place?
- What else was going on when the behavior took place?
- "During the feedback exercise when we were making a decision on..."

9-56

**Slide 9–57**

## Behavior

- Feedback should always describe behavior, not voice a conclusion.
- "You said my idea would not work" or "You smiled at me and made eye contact."
- Not, "You are arrogant," or "You are a nice person."

9-57

**Slide 9–58**

## Impact

- Describe how the behavior affected you or how you perceive it affected others.
- "That caused me to withdraw from the conversation."
- "It made me feel comfortable with the group."

9-58

**Slide 9–59**

## Feedback Should Always Be Well Intentioned

- Effective feedback is meant to help the recipient. It's a gift.
- Don't give "feedback" because you want to "get something off of your chest."
- Feedback will not fix what you believe is wrong with another person.

9-59

**Slide 9–60**

## Avoid Judging Behavior

- Don't use terms such as "good" or "bad."
- The receiver decides the value of the impact of his or her behavior.
- Judging the impact of the receiver's behavior often decreases the receiver's willingness to listen.

9-60

**Slide 9–61**

## Distinguish Feedback from "I Want" Statements

- If you want something, ask for it.
- Say, "I want you to approve my project," rather than "You're holding up my project."
- Avoid passive-aggressive behavior.

9-61

**Slide 9–62**

## Give Information, Not Advice

- The goal of feedback is to help someone understand and accept the impact of his or her behavior on others.
- The goal is NOT to change someone's behavior.
- The recipient's decision to change behavior is not part of the feedback process.

9-62

**Slide 9–63**

## Expect Feedback in Return

- Feedback begets feedback.
- Be a good feedback recipient. Listen and ask clarifying questions, but don't defend or justify behaviors.
- Remember that everyone has a right to his or her own perceptions.

9-63

**Slide 9–64**

## Coach as Guide

American Society for Training & Development

9-64

**Slide 9–65**

## Role

- Help the person you are coaching clarify and articulate his or her personal vision. And…
- Identify points of alignment between his or her personal vision and the organization's vision.
- Set short-term goals that move him or her closer to personal visions.
- Clarify his or her role/task.

9-65

**Slide 9–66**

## Vision…

- Gives a sense of the future
- Guides decisions
- Shapes behavior
- Inspires creativity and energy (creative tension)
- Constantly evolves

9-66

---

*Slide 9–67*

## SMART Goals

- Specific
- Measurable
- Achievable
- Relevant
- Time-bound

9-67

---

*Slide 9–68*

## Values

- Identify the types of behaviors that will be used to pursue the achievement of goals.
  - Integrity
  - Consideration of others
  - Prioritizing conflicting goals

9-68

---

*Slide 9–69*

## Prioritizing Goals

- Consider how achievement of the goal will affect progress toward your vision and...
- How much influence you have over the likelihood the goal will be accomplished and...
- How much risk you are comfortable taking.

9-69

---

*Slide 9–70*

## Prioritizing Goals

|  | Low Impact on Vision | High Impact on Vision |
|---|---|---|
| High Ability to Influence | Conservative | Highest Priority |
| Low Ability to Influence | Lowest Priority | Aggressive |

9-70

---

*Slide 9–71*

## Prioritizing Goals

- Those with an aggressive approach should put goals with a high impact on the vision and low ability to influence as their second-highest priority goals.
- Those with a conservative approach should put goals with a low impact on the vision and high ability to influence as their second-highest priority goals.

9-71

---

*Slide 9–72*

## Clarifying Role/Task

- Identify the scope of the role/task.
- Define role/task by deliverables/outputs.
- Clarify when deliverables are expected.
- Define the resources available to complete the deliverables (human, financial, physical).
- Metrics used to measure accomplishments are the clearest definition of the role/task (what gets measured gets done).

9-72

**Slide 9–73**

## Evaluating Progress

- The process for evaluating a goal can have a tremendous impact on the results of the evaluation.
  - **Who** will be doing the evaluation?
  - **What** will they use as metrics?
  - **How** will they evaluate the metrics?
  - **When** will the evaluation be conducted?

9-73

**Slide 9–74**

## Coach as Teacher

American Society for Training & Development

9-74

**Slide 9–75**

## When "Coaching" Means "Teaching"

- Transferring knowledge
- Transferring ability to perform a task
- Transferring a skill

9-75

**Slide 9–76**

## Teaching a Skill or Process

- Being good at doing something can be very different from articulating *how* to do something.
- Match the teaching approach with the learner's primary learning style.
- Responsibility for learning resides with the learner.

9-76

**Slide 9–77**

## Learning Styles

- Visual/Nonverbal
- Visual/Verbal
- Auditory
- Kinesthetic

9-77

**Slide 9–78**

## Visual/Nonverbal Learners

- Learn best when information is presented visually as a picture or design.
- Use visual aids that include pictures and graphics.
- Help them create mental pictures that represent information.

9-78

**Slide 9–79**

## Look for...

- Affinity for putting jigsaw puzzles together
- Doodling during meetings
- Good at reading maps
- Keen observation
- Interest in art

9-79

**Slide 9–80**

## Visual/Verbal Learners

- Learn best when information is presented visually using letters, words, and phrases.
- Use visual aids that include bullet points, graphs, flowcharts.
- Use worksheets to help them write instructions and process steps in their own words.

9-80

**Slide 9–81**

## Look for...

- Reading books as a favorite pastime
- Enjoyment of crossword puzzles
- Keen observation
- Affinity for printed instructions

9-81

**Slide 9–82**

## Auditory Learners

- Learn best when hearing information that is being presented.
- Use oral presentations.
- Encourage as much verbal interaction as possible.
- Have them repeat key points back to you.

9-82

**Slide 9–83**

## Look for...

- Tendency to ask a lot of questions
- Reading aloud
- Affinity for learning in groups
- A collection of books on tape
- Attentive listening

9-83

**Slide 9–84**

## Kinesthetic Learners

- Learn best when physically engaged in an activity.
- Use "hands-on" learning exercises.
- Incorporate physical activity as much as possible.
- Use physical objects as symbols.
- Encourage repetitive practice of the skill/task.

9-84

## Slide 9–85

Look for...

- Hobbies that involve physical activity such as sports, dancing, or building models
- Short attention span during verbal discussions
- Dislike of sitting still for long periods
- Affinity for solving three-dimensional puzzles

9-85

## Slide 9–86

Coach as Motivator

American Society for Training & Development

9-86

## Slide 9–87

Motivator's Role

- Help the person you are coaching see the bridge between
  - What they value and desire and...
  - The task or role for which they are responsible.
- Encourage belief in his or her ability to be successful.
- Align his or her level of confidence with his or her abilities.

9-87

## Slide 9–88

Value Awareness

- Most people know what is important to them, what they value and desire.
- However, people tend to think of all of their important values as equal, making it hard to make rational trade-offs among values.
- Increased awareness of personal values and their priority of importance leads to greater motivation and more rewarding decisions and behaviors.

9-88

## Slide 9–89

Value Trade-offs

- You are preparing to leave the office for your seven-year-old daughter's championship soccer game when one your most important (and lucrative) clients calls. There is an emergency situation and they need you to work with them for a couple of hours. No on else at the office can meet the client's needs.
- **What do you do?**

9-89

## Slide 9–90

Value Trade-offs

- As you are checking your bills one day you realize that a $500 credit card charge from several months ago was never billed to you.
- **Do you try to rectify the error?**

9-90

**Slide 9–91**

## Confidence

- Optimum results are achieved when ability and confidence are realistically viewed.
- Lack of confidence requires encouraging behaviors.
- Overconfidence requires aligning behaviors.

9-91

**Slide 9–92**

## Encouraging Behaviors

- Recognizing accomplishments, even "small" ones
- Appreciating efforts
- Offering support and assistance
- Being sympathetic to perceived challenges the person is facing
- Validating current levels of accomplishment while advocating greater achievement
- Reinforcing the importance of the task/role
- Smiling

9-92

**Slide 9–93**

## Aligning Behaviors

- Providing specific, timely observations on performance and effectiveness
- Inquiring about the source of their perceived expertise, knowledge, or experience
- Identifying potential challenges, pitfalls, and unforeseen consequences

9-93

**Slide 9–94**

## Coach as Mentor

American Society for Training & Development

9-94

**Slide 9–95**

## What Is Mentoring?

- A deliberate, conscious, voluntary relationship
- A relationship between people who do not generally have a supervisory relationship
- Beneficial to the mentor, person being mentored, and the organization
- Matching the interests and talents of the person being mentored with the organization 's needs and development opportunities.

9-95

**Slide 9–96**

## Role of the Mentor

- Connecting your partner to other members of the organization.
- Sharing your experiences and providing knowledge on the formal and informal processes of the organization.
- Providing career guidance.

9-96

*Slide 9–97*

## Mentoring Tips

- Put yourself in their shoes – What did I want to know when I was in their situation?
- Make mentoring a priority – Meet your commitments (meetings, deliverables, etc.)
- Spend more time listening than advising.
- Maintain confidentiality.
- Stick to what you know. Don't try to be all things to the person you are mentoring.

9-97

*Slide 9–98*

## Mentoring Tips

- Being "right" isn't as important as being understood and accepted.
- Mentoring is not making a clone of yourself.
- Get to know the people you are mentoring: what excites them, what challenges them, what they value.

9-98

*Slide 9–99*

## Mentoring Tips

- Identify the principles that have made you successful and help your partner put those principles to use in the context of his or her skills, personality, and goals.

9-99

# Content Modules

- Detailed instructions for using the content modules
- 11 content modules

This chapter contains all the content modules that appear in the sample agendas found in previous chapters. The term "content" refers to the emphases within the modules. Each content module is a self-contained learning experience that can be used as a standalone training session or incorporated into a broader agenda. The interactive designs explore content areas in step-by-step fashion. They are handy, readily available resources to help trainers address the issues that coaches face.

## Using the Content Modules

These content modules are the building blocks of a training program for coaches. Each module includes, as appropriate:

- step-by-step instructions
- key learning points
- discussion questions
- a list of materials to be used in each module, including
  - training instruments
  - PowerPoint presentations
  - structured exercises.

Trainers should review the content module they are going to facilitate, along with all of the resources used in the module. After becoming familiar with the content, follow the step-by-step instructions for facilitating the module. Time estimates are provided for each module and each step, but the time needed for each activity may vary with different facilitators and participants.

A trainer can modify these modules to comply with the priorities of his or her organization; the readiness level of potential participants; or resources available in terms of time, space, and availability of trainees. These modules implement many of the principles of adult learning specified in chapter 3 of this book. It is important that the trainer understands and is committed to these principles before undertaking revisions of the step-by-step approaches included here.

## The Modules

The designs included in this chapter emphasize learning through doing and use the materials included in this book. As recommended in chapter 2, it's important to conduct a needs assessment before deciding what modules will be used, how they will be modified, and how you will combine various modules into longer sessions.

There are 11 modules in this section:

- ◆ **Content Module 10–1: Learning Partners.** This module helps create a collaborative learning environment by introducing participants to each other and to the idea that each person's role is to contribute to the learning process.

- ◆ **Content Module 10–2: What Is Coaching?** The term "coaching" covers a wide variety of topics. This module covers the importance of properly defining the coaching role.

- ◆ **Content Module 10–3: Coaching Self-Assessment.** This module uses a self-assessment instrument to help participants identify areas in which their learning can have the most impact. It provides a "learning road map" for coaches.

- ◆ **Content Module 10–4: Needs Assessment and Defining the Coaching Relationship.** Having agreement with the person being coached on the role of the coach and the expected outcomes of the coaching process is important to a successful coaching relationship.

This module covers the two-way nature of the coaching relationship and how to align expectations among everyone involved. It also includes an assessment to help with this process.

◆ **Content Module 10–5: Building Trust and Rapport.** The nature of trust is covered in this module, as well as ways to build trust between the coach and person being coached.

◆ **Content Module 10–6: Listening for Understanding.** This module looks at the importance of listening in the coaching role. It also covers techniques for effective listening.

◆ **Content Module 10–7: Giving Effective Feedback.** Principles and techniques for providing effective feedback are covered in this module.

◆ **Content Module 10–8: Coach as Guide.** This module looks at how a coach helps the person being coached to define "success." It includes creating a vision, setting goals, action planning, and evaluating progress.

◆ **Content Module 10–9: Coach as Motivator.** Being an effective motivator involves helping the person you are coaching find meaning in his or her role, task, or assignment. This module also covers building confidence, mitigating over-confidence, and identifying reinforcing consequences.

◆ **Content Module 10–10: Coach as Teacher.** This module covers the process of transferring knowledge or skills to another person. It includes discussion of learning styles and the importance of being able to articulate the discrete steps of a process.

◆ **Content Module 10–11: Coach as Mentor.** This module looks at enabling the person being coached to use his or her personal traits and skills effectively in the context of his or her organization's norms, policies, and culture.

## Content Module 10-1: Learning Partners

This module helps create the learning environment by preparing participants to act as learning partners with each other.

### *TIME*

◆ 10 minutes, plus approximately 3 minutes per participant

### *AGENDA*

◆ Discuss key points. (5 minutes)

◆ Facilitate introduction exercise. (3 minutes per participant)

◆ Review some of the strengths and learning priorities of participants. (5 minutes)

### *KEY POINTS*

◆ Everyone knows something about coaching and can contribute to learning.

◆ One person's development needs are often the strengths of another.

### *INTRODUCTION EXERCISE*

A variety of introduction techniques can be used, based on the time available and the preference of the facilitator. One technique used with success is to have participants pair up and interview each other. Then have each participant introduce his or her interview partner to the group. Information in the introductions should include

◆ name

◆ area or function in which he or she works

◆ how long he or she has been in a coaching role

◆ one thing he or she does well as a coach

◆ one thing he or she would like to learn about being a coach.

# Content Module 10–2: What Is Coaching?

This module helps participants recognize the importance of clearly defining their coaching roles.

## *TIME*

◆  1 hour

## *MATERIALS*

◆  Structured Experience 12–1: What Is Coaching? (chapter 12, page 148)

◆  PowerPoint presentation *What Is Coaching.ppt* (on the CD)

## *AGENDA*

◆  Lead group through the first discussion question below. (5 minutes)

◆  Review PowerPoint presentation "What Is Coaching?" (25 minutes) Discussion questions 2 and 3 are included in the presentation.

◆  Facilitate Structured Experience 12–1: What Is Coaching? (30 minutes)

## *KEY POINTS*

◆  Coaching is helping others succeed through guiding, teaching, motivating, and mentoring.

◆  Coaching takes place within a defined context, such as a specific task, skill, or responsibility.

◆  Done well, coaching can transfer knowledge on a just-in-time basis in our organizations, increase individual motivation and morale, and help organizations deliver outstanding results.

◆  Done poorly, coaching can waste the time of valuable resources, create a hostile work environment, and create suboptimal organizations.

## *DISCUSSION QUESTIONS*

1.  What does coaching mean to you?

2.  Have you ever had a good coach? What was it like?

3.  Have you ever had a bad coach? What was it like?

## Content Module 10–3: Coaching Self-Assessment

This module will help participants recognize learning opportunities that offer the greatest possibility for improving their coaching skills. Identification of these learning leverage points will increase the effectiveness of the training that follows.

### *TIME*

◆ 1 hour

### *MATERIALS*

◆ Assessment 11–2: Coaching Self-Assessment (chapter 11, page 124)

### *AGENDA*

◆ Discuss key points. (5 minutes)

◆ Administer the assessment and have participants review the "Why these competencies are important" section. (15 minutes)

◆ Ask participants to divide into pairs and help each other complete the action plan section. (20 minutes)

◆ Lead entire group through discussion questions. (20 minutes)

### *KEY POINTS*

◆ Successful coaches have a clearly defined coaching role that involves being a guide, teacher, motivator, mentor, or any combination of these roles.

◆ It's important to identify which role or roles your coaching engagement involves and to bring the proper skills to bear.

◆ Knowing your coaching strengths and weaknesses will help you coach more effectively.

### *DISCUSSION QUESTIONS*

1. How can the strengths you identified in the self-assessment help you be an effective coach? (Ask for examples from past experiences.)

2. What can you do to shore up your areas of need?

## Content Module 10–4: Needs Assessment and Defining the Coaching Relationship

This module will help coaches identify the highest leverage coaching needs of the person they are coaching, define the nature of their coaching engagement, and ensure that all parties involved have a common understanding of the expected outcomes of the coaching engagement.

### TIME

♦ 2 hours

### MATERIALS

♦ Assessment 11–6: Coaching Needs Assessment (chapter 11, page 137)

♦ Training Instrument 11–1: Coaching Agreements Worksheet (chapter 11, page 141)

♦ Structured Experience 12–2: I Want to Drive (chapter 12, page 149)

♦ PowerPoint presentations *Assessing Coaching Needs.ppt* and *Defining the Coaching Relationship.ppt* (on the CD)

### AGENDA

♦ Lead participants through discussion question 1. (5 minutes)

♦ Introduce and hand out the "Coaching Needs Assessment." (5 minutes)

♦ Review the PowerPoint presentation "Assessing Coaching Needs." (30 minutes)

♦ Discuss the key points. Lead participants through discussion questions 2 and 3. (10 minutes)

♦ Review the PowerPoint presentation "Defining the Coaching Relationship." (10 minutes)

♦ Facilitate the "I Want to Drive" structured experience. (1 hour)

### *KEY POINTS*

- Some coaching assignments are fairly specific:

    - Teach John to post journal entries.

    - Act as a mentor to the newly hired management intern.

- Use the "Coaching Needs Assessment" if the nature of the coaching engagement is not clearly defined.

- The coaching process should be a journey of shared discovery and learning. The coach can learn as much as the person being coached.

- Aligned expectations of the coach, the person being coached, and, if applicable, the supervisor of the coach or person being coached are critical to a successful coaching engagement.

### *DISCUSSION QUESTIONS*

1. Think of when you were someone's coach. Did you act more as a guide, teacher, motivator, or mentor?

2. What concerns do you have about being a coach?

3. What excites you about being a coach?

# Content Module 10–5:
# Building Trust and Rapport

This module discusses the importance of defining the boundaries of trust in a relationship and looks at ways to build trust between the coach and the person being coached.

## TIME

◆ 2.25 hours

## MATERIALS

◆ Structured Experience 12–3: Building Rapport (chapter 12, page 151)

◆ Structured Experience 12–4: Trust Walk (chapter 12, page 153)

◆ PowerPoint presentation *Building Trust and Rapport.ppt* (on the CD)

## AGENDA

◆ Lead group through discussion question 1. (10 minutes)

◆ Present key points, using the PowerPoint presentation "Building Trust and Rapport." Discussion question 2 is included in the presentation. (20 minutes)

◆ Facilitate the "Building Rapport" structured experience. (1 hour)

◆ Facilitate the "Trust Walk" structured experience. (45 minutes)

## KEY POINTS

◆ There are two aspects of trust:

   ◆ *Trust in another's motivation.* (Do their intentions align with yours?)

   ◆ *Trust in another's competence.* (Do they have the ability to carry out those intentions?) For example, I may trust my spouse's intentions toward me in all situations, but I wouldn't trust him or her to work on my car.

◆ Trust is most easily established when the boundaries of that trust are clearly defined. No one deserves universal trust that would apply in all situations.

- Trust helps build healthy relationships when the truster and trustee share a common understanding of the boundaries. This keeps misunderstandings and unmet expectations to a minimum.

- Strategies for building trust:

  - *Trust begets trust.* Showing trust to another person makes it more likely he or she will trust you.

  - *Self-disclosure.* Judiciously disclosing personal or private information demonstrates trust. Be careful not to disclose too much or you can make the other person feel uncomfortable and cause distrust.

  - *Make eye contact.* The eyes have been called the "windows to the soul." Making occasional eye contact can help someone else feel he or she can trust you.

  - *Honor the existing situation.* Coaching relationships are often intended to create change on the part of the person being coached. It's important for the coach to show honor and respect for the current state before pushing for change.

  - *Show how the self-interests of all parties involved are in alignment.* Most people are comfortable trusting someone else to pursue his or her own self-interest.

- People are more alike than different, and relationships are strengthened when we focus on similarities. The key is to focus on something you respect in the other person whenever you interact with them. For example, you may not respect someone's ability to manage others, but you may respect their devotion to their children. Focus on how you see them as a parent when you interact with them and they will sense and respond to your respect.

## DISCUSSION QUESTIONS

1. Is it important for the person you are coaching to trust you? Why?

2. What are some ways to build trust in a relationship?

# Content Module 10–6: Listening for Understanding

This module looks at the importance of listening in the coaching role. It also covers techniques for effective listening.

## TIME

◆ 1.75 hours

## MATERIALS

◆ Assessment 11–7: Listening Self-Assessment (chapter 11, page 139)

◆ Structured Experience 12–5: Draw It (chapter 12, page 155)

◆ PowerPoint presentation *Listening for Understanding.ppt* (on the CD)

## AGENDA

◆ Lead group through discussion questions 1 and 2. (10 minutes)

◆ Administer the "Listening Self-Assessment." (10 minutes) Let participants know they will learn more about how to address their results during the PowerPoint presentation.

◆ Present key points using the PowerPoint presentation "Listening for Understanding." (15 minutes)

◆ Facilitate participants through discussion question 3. (10 minutes)

◆ Facilitate the "Draw It" structured experience. (1 hour)

## KEY POINTS

◆ There are three aspects of effective listening:

1. *Focus:* Paying complete attention to the speaker and the message he or she is trying to convey. Many people consider this critical to being a good listener, but it's not enough.

2. *Feedback:* Actively engaging the speaker through encouraging words and gestures, clarifying questions, and summarizing key points. Listening is part of the cycle of communicating. The listener is as responsible as the speaker for making sure effective communication takes place.

3. *Filtering:* Creating personal meaning from the speaker's comments. Putting the speaker's comments in context with your own experiences, knowledge, and perceptions. This is difficult to control, but listeners should be aware of how filtering can affect communication.

◆ Tips to help listeners keep focused:

   ◆ *Face the speaker.* Eyes and ears are designed to pick up what is directly in front of our faces.

   ◆ *Make eye contact.* This keeps the listener engaged and looking at the speaker's face for cues. It also encourages the speaker and indicates that you are listening.

   ◆ *Don't let your brain outrun the conversation.* Most listeners think faster than a speaker can talk. This is one reason people's minds wander when listening, especially to extended speeches. In order to keep their minds from wandering, listeners should use their "excess" thinking capacity to think about issues related to the conversation.

   ◆ *Pay attention to both verbal and physical cues.* This helps the listener stay focused and engaged.

   ◆ *Take your time in responding.* Pressure to respond quickly leads to thinking of a response instead of listening.

◆ Tips for using feedback in effective listening:

   ◆ *Verbal*

      ◆ Ask clarifying questions to keep assumptions to a minimum.

      ◆ Restate or paraphrase comments from the speaker to check for common understanding.

      ◆ Use such listening comments as, "I see," "uh-huh," or "oh really," to encourage the speaker and let him or her know you are engaged.

      ◆ Summarize facts, feelings conveyed, or other key points to check for agreement.

      ◆ Don't interrupt the speaker to make listening comments, paraphrases, or summaries. Wait for an appropriate break in his or her speaking rhythm.

- *Nonverbal*

  - Face the speaker.

  - Maintain eye contact, while being sensitive to the speaker's comfort with the amount of eye contact.

  - Adopt a listening posture by assuming a relaxed body posture and leaning discreetly toward the speaker.

  - Change your posture if you find your attention drifting.

  - Keep arms at your side or hands in your lap.

- Tips for controlling mental filters while listening:

  - *Concentrate on what the speaker is trying to say.* Effective listeners don't mentally argue or judge a speaker's comments until he or she has finished speaking.

  - *Avoid emotional reactions until the conversation is complete.* Emotional reactions during conversations can lead to hearing what you want or expect to hear, not what the speaker is actually trying to say. Try to remain objective.

  - *Be judicious in anticipating statements.* Although anticipating what the speaker will say next can keep you engaged in the conversation, it can also color your view of what the speaker actually says if it differs from what you thought the speaker would say.

- The power of silence is a useful listening tool to elicit more in-depth information:

  - Silence during a conversation is uncomfortable, and people feel compelled to break it.

  - If you are silent but engaged (maintain eye contact and listening posture), the other person will usually volunteer more information on whatever topic is being addressed. This is especially effective when the person may be reluctant to provide information.

## DISCUSSION QUESTIONS

1. Think of a really good coach. Do you think of that person as a good listener?

2.  Have you had a coach who was a poor listener? How did that affect his or her effectiveness as a coach?

3.  Which aspect of listening do you think causes the most misunderstandings?

## Content Module 10–7: Giving Effective Feedback

This module covers the principles and techniques for providing effective feedback.

### TIME

- 2–2.5 hours

### MATERIALS

- Training Instrument 11–2: Feedback Preparation Worksheet (chapter 11, page 142)

- Structured Experience 12–6: Team Theater (chapter 12, page 159)

- PowerPoint presentation *Effective Feedback.ppt* (on the CD)

### AGENDA

- Lead the group through discussion questions 1 and 2. (10 minutes)

- Review the key points using the PowerPoint presentation "Effective Feedback." (15 minutes)

- Facilitate the "Team Theater" structured experience. (1.5–2 hours)

### KEY POINTS

- Feedback cannot be forced on someone; it must be voluntarily accepted.

- The goal of feedback is to help someone understand and accept the impact of his or her behavior on others. It is *not* to change someone's behavior. It is *not* giving advice. Any behavior change is up to the feedback recipient.

- Feedback that labels behavior as "good" or "bad" is uncomfortable to give and receive. Feedback that judges behavior is more likely to be ineffective, offensive, or destructive.

- Using the situation-behavior-impact model for providing feedback can make it easier to provide effective feedback.

## *DISCUSSION QUESTIONS*

**1.** Think of someone you know who is good at giving feedback. What makes him or her effective?

**2.** Are most people comfortable giving feedback? Why?

# Content Module 10–8: Coach as Guide

This module looks at how a coach helps the person being coached define "success." It includes creating a vision, setting goals, planning action, and evaluating progress.

## TIME

- ◆ 1.5 hours

## MATERIALS

- ◆ Structured Experience 12–7: Where Do I Want to Go? (chapter 12, page 162)

- ◆ PowerPoint presentation *Coach as Guide.ppt* (on the CD)

## AGENDA

- ◆ Lead the group through discussion question 1. (5 minutes)

- ◆ Present the key points using the PowerPoint presentation "Coach as Guide." (25 minutes)

- ◆ Facilitate the "Where Do I Want to Go?" experience. (1 hour)

## KEY POINTS

- ◆ The coach's role as guide is to help the person he or she is coaching find the alignment between his or her personal vision and the organization's vision, and then help him or her set goals to move closer to that vision.

- ◆ Creative tension is necessary to create energy and innovation and only exists to the extent the person's vision for the future is significantly different from his or her current circumstances. The gap between future vision and current circumstances drives behaviors to close the gap.

- ◆ Vision provides a sense of the future, guides decisions, shapes behavior, inspires creativity and energy, and constantly evolves.

- ◆ Well-defined goals are **SMART:**

    - ◆ **Specific.** Like ordering a meal in a restaurant, the more specific you are about what you want, the more likely you are to get it.

- **Measurable.** In order to confirm progress, goals need to be measurable. Visible progress can be a motivating factor.

- **Achievable.** If a goal is such a stretch that it looks unrealistic or unachievable, it can be demoralizing.

- **Relevant.** Goals should have a direct tie to the organizational or personal vision.

- **Time-bound.** Deadlines are great motivators.

◆ Values identify the types of behaviors that will be used to achieve the goals.

◆ Prioritizing goals is effective when considering both the ability to influence accomplishment of the goal and the impact the accomplishment of the goal will have on achieving the vision.

◆ A well-defined task or role includes clearly identified scope, deliverables, deadlines, resources, and metrics.

◆ The process for evaluating a goal can have a tremendous impact on the results of the evaluation. Planning for evaluation of goals should consider the following:

- Who will be doing the evaluation? What is his or her point of view?

- What will he or she use as metrics? Are the metrics objective?

- How will he or she evaluate the metrics? Are there multiple ways to evaluate the metrics? Will these produce differing results?

- When will the evaluation be conducted? Is the timeframe for evaluation clear and commonly understood?

## DISCUSSION QUESTIONS

1. What do you want your life to be like in 10 years? (Components of a future vision often include where people live, where they work, the type of work they do, the position they hold at work, their family circumstances, their relationships, their wealth accumulation, and their physical status.)

2. How is that different from today?

# Content Module 10–9: Coach as Motivator

This module covers building confidence, mitigating overconfidence, and identifying reinforcing consequences.

## *TIME*

- ◆ 1.5 hours

## *MATERIALS*

- ◆ Structured Experience 12–11: What's Important to Me? (chapter 12, page 175)

- ◆ PowerPoint presentation *Coach as Motivator.ppt* (on CD)

## *AGENDA*

- ◆ Lead the group through discussion question 1. (5 minutes)

- ◆ Present the key points using the PowerPoint presentation "Coach as Motivator." (25 minutes) Discussion questions 2 and 3 are included in the presentation.

- ◆ Facilitate the "What's Important to Me?" exercise. (1 hour)

## *KEY POINTS*

- ◆ People do what they think they need to do to get what they think they want.

- ◆ Coaches can assist by helping the person being coached understand what he or she wants and how the task or role for which he or she is responsible will help in acquiring that.

- ◆ Increased awareness of personal values and their priority of importance leads to greater motivation and more rewarding decisions and behaviors.

- ◆ Both lack of confidence and overconfidence can create ineffective behaviors.

## *DISCUSSION QUESTIONS*

1.  What can someone else do to motivate you?

2. You are preparing to leave the office for your seven-year-old daughter's championship soccer game when one of your most important (and lucrative) clients calls. The client has an emergency situation and needs you to work on it for a couple of hours. No one else at the office can meet the client's needs. What do you do?

3. As you are checking your bills one day you realize that a $500 credit card charge from several months ago was never billed to you. Would you try to rectify the error?

# Content Module 10–10: Coach as Teacher

This module covers how to transfer knowledge effectively to another person. The content includes how to break a process down into discrete steps and how to identify and work with various learning styles.

## TIME

◆ 2.5–3.5 hours

## MATERIALS

◆ Structured Experience 12–8: Break it Down (chapter 12, page 164)

◆ Structured Experience 12–9: Origami Knowledge Transfer (chapter 12, page 166, and on the CD)

◆ Structured Experience 12–10: Snowflake (chapter 12, page 172)

◆ PowerPoint presentation *Coach as Teacher.ppt* (on the CD)

## AGENDA

◆ Lead the group through discussion question 1. (10 minutes)

◆ Discuss the first two key points. (5 minutes)

◆ Facilitate the "Break It Down" structured experience. (1 hour)

◆ Present the remaining key points using the PowerPoint presentation "Coach as Teacher." (15 minutes)

◆ Facilitate the "Origami Knowledge Transfer" experience. (1 hour)

◆ Facilitate the "Snowflake" exercise for larger groups. (1 hour)

## KEY POINTS

◆ Most coaches are selected to teach because they have demonstrated expertise or knowledge. However, expertise does not necessarily translate into ability to teach.

◆ The first step in being able to teach a topic or skill is being able to articulate knowledge in such a way that others can understand it.

◆ There are different approaches to learning, known as learning styles:

- ◆ visual/nonverbal

- ◆ visual/verbal

- ◆ auditory

- ◆ kinesthetic.

- ◆ Each person has a primary learning style that works best for him or her.

- ◆ Teaching is most effective when it is conducted with consideration for the learner's primary learning style.

- ◆ Responsibility for learning always resides with the learner.

 **DISCUSSION QUESTION**

1. Who was the best teacher you ever had? What made him or her effective?

# Content Module 10–11: Coach as Mentor

This module looks at enabling the person you are coaching to use his or her personal traits and skills effectively in the context of the organization's norms, policies, and culture.

## TIME

◆ 1 hour

## MATERIALS

◆ Structured Experience 12–12: Mentoring Discussion (chapter 12, page 177)

◆ PowerPoint presentation *Coach as Mentor.ppt* (on the CD)

## AGENDA

◆ Lead the group through discussion question 1. (5 minutes)

◆ Present the key points using the PowerPoint presentation "Coach as Mentor." (15 minutes)

◆ Facilitate the "Mentoring Discussion" structured experience. (40 minutes)

## KEY POINTS

◆ A mentoring relationship should be voluntary because it requires a great deal of trust that cannot be forced.

◆ The mentor's role is to match the interests and talents of the person he or she is mentoring with the organization's needs and development opportunities.

◆ The key to a successful mentoring relationship is *not* the degree of similarity between the mentor and the partner, but the mentor's ability to relate to, understand, and accept what the partner is experiencing.

◆ Being "right" isn't as important as being understood and accepted. Suggesting an approach that isn't 100 percent the way you would do it but that would be more enthusiastically embraced by the person you are mentoring may be the most effective approach. If he or she will take to heart an "almost right" suggestion, that's far better than rejecting the "perfect" solution.

◆ Being "right" isn't necessarily being like you. Mentoring is not making a clone of yourself.

◆ The mentor must get to know the person he or she is mentoring: what excites him or her, what challenges him or her, and what he or she values.

◆ Identify the principles that have made you successful and help the person you are mentoring put those principles to use in the context of his or her skills, personality, and goals. Much like Stephen Covey did in his *Seven Habits of Highly Effective People*, mentors should try to identify their "seven habits."

 ### *DISCUSSION QUESTION*

1. What does "mentoring" mean to you?

◆

# Assessments and Training Instruments

**What's in This Chapter?**

- ◆ Instructions for using assessments and instruments
- ◆ Seven assessments
- ◆ Four training instruments

There are many worksheets and data-gathering instruments available to the trainer who is working with coaches. This chapter includes assessments and training instruments that rate relevant traits, competencies, and practices, as well as other tools to assist in the learning process.

An assessment differs from a test in that the answers to the questions are not considered right or wrong. Most of the assessments are designed to elicit self-perceptions. The increased self-awareness from the self-assessment process helps participants focus on learning objectives to which they can willingly commit.

*A note on reliability and validity:* The major consideration regarding these training instruments is usefulness, not predictive power. They have not been tested for reliability or validity, but were designed primarily to generate data for action planning and personal commitment and to promote learning about what is important.

The training instruments were designed to be used as training tools, and some can be used by participants during the actual coaching process.

## Assessments and Training Instruments

- ◆ **Assessment 11–1: Structured Interview Protocol for Assessing the Learning Needs of Coaches.** When you meet with individuals and groups to assess their learning needs, it is important to operate in an organized way. This is a protocol for conducting such exchanges.

- **Assessment 11–2: Coaching Self-Assessment.** This self-assessment helps participants understand the competencies required to be a good coach and makes it easy for them to set developmental priorities and plans.

- **Assessment 11–3: Needs Assessment Focus Group Discussion Sheet.** This sheet helps participants prepare for the focus group discussion.

- **Assessment 11–4: Trainer Competencies.** This form helps you establish learning priorities for your own development as a trainer. It can be used as a self-assessment or to solicit feedback from trainees at the end of a session or some time later.

- **Assessment 11–5: Coaching Training Follow-Up Assessment.** This questionnaire is designed to find out how coaches change behaviors after attending training. It is best to wait a few months after the training before carrying out the research.

- **Assessment 11–6: Coaching Needs Assessment.** This assessment will help the coach determine the most important needs of the person he or she is coaching, based on discussions and observations.

- **Assessment 11–7: Listening Self-Assessment.** The results of this assessment will help direct and focus the efforts of participants in improving their listening skills. This assessment reviews how adept participants are at three key aspects of effective listening.

- **Training Instrument 11–1: Coaching Agreements Worksheet.** This worksheet is used in the "I Want to Drive" structured experience. It assists in capturing the agreements between the coach and person being coached regarding definitions of success, commitments, and expectations.

- **Training Instrument 11–2: Feedback Preparation Worksheet.** This worksheet is used in the "Team Theater" structured experience. It assists participants in preparing feedback to give to others prior to a feedback or coaching session.

◆ **Training Instrument 11–3: Process Steps Worksheet.** This worksheet is used in the "Break It Down" structured experience. Participants use this worksheet to create step-by-step documentation of a process.

◆ **Training Instrument 11–4: Values Worksheet.** This worksheet is used in the "What's Important to Me?" structured experience. It provides a process for identifying the participants' value priorities.

---

*Assessment 11–1*

**Structured Interview Protocol for Assessing the Learning Needs of Coaches**

*Instructions:* Use this form for taking notes during interviews with newly appointed coaches in order to assess their developmental needs. Make certain you understand the person's response to each question before writing a summary of what he or she says. Assure the interviewee that the responses will be both anonymous and confidential.

1. How did you become a coach?

2. What competencies did management see in you before appointing you as a coach?

3. What concerns, if any, did management tell you about as you became a coach?

4. In your coaching role, what concerns do you have?

5. What do you especially like about being a coach?

6. What do you see as your primary strengths as a coach?

7. What is your most common source of stress in your role as coach?

*Continued on next page*

*Assessment 11–1, continued*
**Structured Interview Protocol for Assessing the Learning Needs of Coaches**

8. What do you think you could improve in yourself as a coach?

9. How interested are you in receiving training in how to coach effectively?

10. How would you describe your relationship with the person you are coaching?

11. What preferences do you have about how you might receive coaching training?

12. How might you "sell" your plan for self-development as a coach to your manager in order to get his or her support?

13. What else can you tell me about your needs for training at this time?

14. What questions do you have about me?

End the interview by thanking the person for his or her candid responses to your questions. Reassure the coach that what is said will not be quoted by name, just combined with others' responses to analyze common themes. Explain that the training for coaches will reflect the priorities of those interviewed.

### Assessment 11-2
### Coaching Self-Assessment

*Instructions:* The purpose of this activity is to assist you in learning about what you need to be successful as a coach and to help you create an action plan for self-improvement. Write an **X** in one of the boxes to the right of each competency, depending on how you see yourself right now. Obviously, you need to be honest with yourself on this. No one will see your ratings unless you voluntarily share them.

| | ONE OF MY STRENGTHS | DOING OKAY ON THIS | NEED TO DEVELOP THIS MORE | DEFINITELY NEED TO DEVELOP THIS |
|---|---|---|---|---|
| **Communicating Instructions**<br>Showing the person you are coaching how to accomplish the task and clarifying when, where, how much, and to what standard it should be done. | ☐ | ☐ | ☐ | ☐ |
| **Setting Performance Goals**<br>Collaborating with others to establish short- and long-term goals for performance on particular tasks. | ☐ | ☐ | ☐ | ☐ |
| **Providing Feedback**<br>Carefully observing performance on individual tasks and sharing these observations in a nonthreatening manner. | ☐ | ☐ | ☐ | ☐ |
| **Rewarding Improvement**<br>Using a variety of means to provide positive reinforcement to others for making progress on the accomplishment of important tasks. | ☐ | ☐ | ☐ | ☐ |
| **Dealing with Failure**<br>Working with others to encourage them when they do not meet expectations. | ☐ | ☐ | ☐ | ☐ |
| **Working with Personal Issues**<br>Listening empathically and without judgment, and offering emotional support for nonwork difficulties. | ☐ | ☐ | ☐ | ☐ |

*Continued on next page*

## Assessment 11–2, continued
### Coaching Self-Assessment

| | ONE OF MY STRENGTHS | DOING OKAY ON THIS | NEED TO DEVELOP THIS MORE | DEFINITELY NEED TO DEVELOP THIS |
|---|---|---|---|---|
| **Confronting Difficult Situations** | ☐ | ☐ | ☐ | ☐ |
| Raising uncomfortable topics that are affecting task accomplishment. | | | | |
| **Responding to Requests** | ☐ | ☐ | ☐ | ☐ |
| Consulting with others on an as-needed basis. Responding to requests in a timely manner. | | | | |
| **Following Through** | ☐ | ☐ | ☐ | ☐ |
| Keeping your commitments. Monitoring outcomes of the coaching process and providing additional assistance when necessary. | | | | |
| **Listening for Understanding** | ☐ | ☐ | ☐ | ☐ |
| Demonstrating attention to and conveying understanding of others. | | | | |
| **Motivating Others** | ☐ | ☐ | ☐ | ☐ |
| Encouraging others to achieve desired results. Creating enthusiasm and commitment in others. | | | | |
| **Assessing Strengths and Weaknesses** | ☐ | ☐ | ☐ | ☐ |
| Identifying root causes of individual performance. Probing beneath the surface of problems. Keenly observing people and events. Defining and articulating issues effectively. | | | | |
| **Building Rapport and Trust** | ☐ | ☐ | ☐ | ☐ |
| Showing respect for others. Acting with integrity and honesty. Easily building bonds with others. Making others feel their concerns and contributions are important. | | | | |

*Continued on next page*

---

*Assessment 11–2, continued*

**Coaching Self-Assessment**

Study this and the following pages to see why those 13 competencies are important for coaches. Then outline an action plan for self-improvement on the final page. Make sure it is a plan to which you are completely committed.

**Why These Competencies Are Important**

The 13 competencies that make up this assessment are of particular importance for those with a coaching role. They represent areas in which you need to excel in order to fulfill your coaching role successfully.

- ◆ **Communicating Instructions.** Showing the person you are coaching how to accomplish the task and clarifying when, where, how much, and to what standard it should be done.

  The role of coach often involves teaching a skill or procedure to another person. The ability to break down a task into easy-to-understand steps that you can articulate to another is vital to being an effective coach.

- ◆ **Setting Performance Goals.** Collaborating with others to establish short- and long-term goals for performance on particular tasks.

  Effective coaching sometimes starts with pointing someone in the right direction. First, you work with the person to set broad goals; then you become very specific in agreeing on desired outcomes and how they will be measured.

- ◆ **Providing Feedback.** Carefully observing performance on individual tasks and sharing these observations in a nonthreatening manner.

  Giving others feedback on their task performance is critical to improving their performance. In order to do this effectively, you have to observe the person performing the task, noting what the person is doing well and what can be improved. Then you work with the individual to ensure he or she understands your feedback and uses it developmentally.

- ◆ **Rewarding Improvement.** Using a variety of means to provide positive reinforcement to others for making progress on the accomplishment of important tasks.

  Timing of rewards is important. Don't wait until you see either perfection or failure on the task. Look for growth in task accomplishment and reward that soon after you observe it. Although coaches don't always control formal rewards (pay, perks, or promotions), they can make frequent and effective use of informal ("pat on the back" or other nonmonetary recognition) ones.

- ◆ **Dealing with Failure.** Working with others to encourage them when they do not meet expectations.

  When an individual demonstrates an inability or unwillingness to perform a task according to expectations and standards, you need to be able to deal with the result. This can mean encouraging, reprimanding, redirecting, retraining, or otherwise

*Continued on next page*

## Assessment 11–2, continued
### Coaching Self-Assessment

affecting his or her ability or willingness. Patience can be a virtue or an enabler of more failure. Use it wisely.

◆ **Working with Personal Issues.** Listening empathically and without judgment and offering emotional support for nonwork difficulties.

In general, coaches are not expected to function as counselors or psychotherapists. Few are qualified to carry out such responsibilities, and the context of the organizational relationship might preclude this type of interaction. Faced with an individual whose personal situation is interfering with his or her performance, however, you need to be able to intervene. A good rule of thumb is that whenever you feel "in over your head," you are. Be prepared to refer the person to appropriate sources of professional assistance and adjust the coaching process to support getting through the situation humanely.

◆ **Confronting Difficult Situations.** Raising uncomfortable topics that are affecting task accomplishment.

Coaching often involves situations in which performance has not met expectations. Unmet expectations often lead to fingerpointing, denial of personal responsibility, and other dysfunctional behaviors. Talking about these issues can make people uncomfortable. Good coaching requires the ability and willingness to confront difficult and uncomfortable situations head-on, but with tact and diplomacy. When the best interests of all concerned are at heart, the honesty and courage to confront difficult situations are welcomed.

◆ **Responding to Requests.** Consulting with others on an as-needed basis. Responding to requests in a timely manner.

Timely response to requests is a tangible indicator of respect. To build and maintain a healthy coaching relationship, make sure your responsiveness reflects a high level of priority.

◆ **Following Through.** Keeping your commitments. Monitoring outcomes of the coaching process and providing additional assistance when necessary.

Trust is a critical component of any coaching relationship. Keeping your commitments helps build and maintain trust. Showing an ongoing commitment to the long-term success of the person you are coaching also builds a strong relationship.

◆ **Listening for Understanding.** Demonstrating attention to and conveying understanding of others.

Listening is another indicator of respect. It requires keeping your mind open to what others say, attending well to both the content of what they say and the feelings they may be expressing (sometimes unconsciously). Listening effectively almost invariably involves checking your understanding of others' messages by reflecting what you hear, using such phrases as, "What I hear you saying is . . . " and, "You seem to be concerned about. . . . "

*Continued on next page*

*Assessment 11–2, continued*
**Coaching Self-Assessment**

- **Motivating Others.** Encouraging others to achieve desired results. Creating enthusiasm and commitment in others.

  The right button to push to help motivate another person differs widely. There are no hard-and-fast rules to what motivates anyone. You can be effective by knowing what motivates the person you are coaching and tying his or her desires and goals to the task at hand. This requires continual assessment and reassessment of the person and situation. "Reading" the person can be inaccurate. It's better to ask what is important to him or her and how the task at hand relates.

- **Assessing Strengths and Weaknesses.** Identifying root causes of individual performance. Probing beneath the surface of problems. Keenly observing people and events. Defining and articulating issues effectively.

  Properly identifying the abilities and interests of the person you are coaching directs your coaching efforts to the most critical areas. This involves keen observation and attention to detail. It also means distinguishing between symptoms and root causes of problems. Without accurate assessment, your coaching efforts might all be spent on addressing the wrong problem or a nonexistent one.

- **Building Rapport and Trust.** Showing respect for others. Acting with integrity and honesty. Easily building bonds with others.

  Making others feel their concerns and contributions are important. Rapport and trust are the cornerstones of an effective coaching relationship. The person you are coaching needs to trust that you have his or her best interests at heart so he or she can be honest with you regarding shortcomings. There also needs to be a bond of mutual respect so the advice, teaching, and counseling of the coach will be more readily accepted.

*Continued on next page*

### *Assessment 11–2, continued*
### *Coaching Self-Assessment*

**Coach's Plan for Self-Improvement**

1. Which, if any, of these competencies are especially relevant to your particular coaching role (guide, teacher, motivator, mentor)?

2. Which two or three competency areas do you need to improve most?

3. What's in it for you to better yourself in these areas?

4. What have you tried before?

5. What steps can you take personally to improve in these areas?

6. What support do you need to improve in these competencies?

7. How will you monitor your progress in self-improvement as a coach?

8. Who needs to know about this?

9. How will you tell him or her?

10. What are your first few steps?

---

*Assessment 11–3*

**Needs Assessment Focus Group Discussion Sheet**

*Instructions:* Use this sheet to prepare for the focus group discussion. Write your first thoughts in response to each question. You may make any changes you wish to your responses during this focus group session. Do not write your name on this sheet. The facilitator will collect the copies of this form at the end of the session.

◆ How would you define the purpose of your coaching role?

◆ What challenges have you had to meet that you didn't expect?

◆ What are you doing particularly well as a coach?

◆ What do you think is the toughest part of being a coach?

◆ What do you think you need help in learning how to do better?

◆ How receptive would you be toward receiving training in the skills you think you need to develop as a coach?

◆ How receptive would you be toward one-on-one assistance to build yourself up as a coach?

◆ How do you prefer that training be offered to you? *(Circle one letter.)*
   a. Group sessions lasting two days
   b. One-day group sessions
   c. Half-day group sessions
   d. Private, individual instruction
   e. No preference

Thank you for your cooperation in this needs assessment.

## *Assessment 11–4*
### Trainer Competencies

This assessment instrument will help you manage your own professional development, and increase the effectiveness of your training sessions with coaches. Trainers can use this instrument in the following ways:

◆ **Self-assessment.** Rating oneself on the five-point scale generates an overall profile and helps isolate the two or three competency areas that are in the greatest need of improvement.

◆ **End-of-course feedback.** Soliciting ratings from trainees can mitigate any tendency trainers may have to deceive themselves in regard to these vital competencies. Trainees may not be able to rate trainers on all 13, so it may be important to ask them to rate only ones for which they consider themselves qualified to provide accurate feedback.

◆ **Observer feedback.** Trainers can observe each other's training activities and provide highly useful information on this set of competencies that are vital to be effective in training coaches.

◆ **Repeat ratings.** This instrument can form the basis for tracking professional growth on the vital few competencies needed to work effectively in developing coaches. The repeat measures can be obtained as often as trainers need in order to inform them of progress on their action plans for improvement.

### The Competencies

Training people who have coaching roles represents a real challenge. The trainer must be good at many things to make such training hit the target. This brief instrument contains a set of 12 vital competencies that this training requires. Of course, not all seasoned trainers are expert in all of these areas, but they represent learning and growth goals for almost any trainer.

Here is the rationale for the importance of each of the dozen critical dimensions of trainer competence.

◆ **Facilitation:** Leads group discussion without directing the outcome. Creates an environment of openness and trust.

Because debriefing experiential learning activities involves group discussion, it is vital that the trainer is competent in initiating, guiding, drawing out, and summarizing such interchanges. It is equally important that the trainer stay out of the content of this give-and-take, carefully avoiding any tendency to manipulate trainees to come up with "right" answers. Experiential learning is learning through discovery, not proving points by the trainer. Trainees need to trust themselves, their experiences, and the trainer to generate learning. The trainer needs to promote an evenness of participation so that all trainees actively seek learning through common activities and debriefings. There is an old saying: "Training goes to where the trainer is coming from." Trainers need to be vigilant so the process of learning does not deteriorate into indoctrination.

*Continued on next page*

## Assessment 11–4, continued
**Trainer Competencies**

◆ **Communication:** Speaks clearly and expresses self well in public settings. Entertains and engages the listener. Conveys ideas in terms the listener can understand.

It is almost axiomatic that trainers should be skilled communicators. This involves entertaining, energetic speech; accurate empathy with trainees; unambiguous self-expression; clear directions for learning activities; and the developed ability to build on the ideas of others. The trainer should be the most competent communicator in the training room. The trainer should be a role model for coaches regarding making messages clear.

◆ **Listening:** Demonstrates attention to and conveys understanding of others.

This is the core communication competency. It involves not only attending to facts and points of view but also feelings, attitudes, and nuances. Any time the trainer does not understand what a trainee is saying or "where the trainee is coming from," the process must be slowed down to generate common meaning. No one listens perfectly. Learning to listen in a highly effective manner is a lifelong quest.

◆ **Coaching:** Assesses strengths and weaknesses of others. Gives timely, specific, constructive feedback.

Working with coaches one-on-one requires that the trainer create opportunities to observe them at work with others. It also entails enrolling them in self-assessment activities, such as using paper-and-pencil instrumentation. A brief tool designed especially for this task, Coaching Self-Assessment, is included in this book. Others, such as their managers, peers, and direct reports, can also use the instrument to provide feedback to coaches. Using such data as these greatly enriches the one-on-one experience because it focuses coaches on what is important and can be repeated to track growth. Coaching can be thought of as individual training, and it is highly specific to the individual trainee. Trainers need to develop high levels of competency in the skills that make up this data-driven development activity.

◆ **Sensitivity to others:** Recognizes feelings, attitudes, and concerns of others.

Because coaches often have emotions that can interfere with their effectiveness, it is vital that the trainer be competent in "reading" them. This involves separating the trainer's inner state from that of the individuals being trained. It also means paying close attention continuously to what trainees are experiencing at the emotional and attitudinal levels. The trainer may or may not draw attention to these inner dynamics, but it is vital to be competent in monitoring them and adjusting the training accordingly.

◆ **Managing conflict:** Identifies sources of conflict. Uses conflict as a constructive process to exchange ideas. Keeps energy focused on desired outcomes.

Sometimes conflict arises in the training room, and the trainer needs to be competent in managing it constructively. The goal is not to resolve the conflict because often there is no real resolution possible, but the aim should be to work with it so as to produce useful learning about how to manage it by responding effectively in real

*Continued on next page*

## Assessment 11–4, *continued*
### Trainer Competencies

time. This is a competency area that signals the trainer's comfort level. If the trainer tends to avoid conflict, the training can become problematic. At worst, it can evolve into a win–lose scenario. It is vital that the trainer recognize the potential for conflict in training coaches and be ready, willing, and able to work with it in a modeling way.

◆ **Influence:** Persuades others to consider a desired point of view. Gains support and commitment from others. Effects change in behavior of others.

Although trainers are not indoctrinators, they often are expected to help coaches understand and accept organizational realities and effective practices. Trainers need to have this competency. They need to be convincing, and they need to be able to "sell" not only the organization's culture but also active participation in experiential learning activities. Highly competent trainers generate genuine commitment from trainees to change their behavior.

◆ **Time management:** Sets efficient work priorities. Can work on many tasks simultaneously. Balances importance and urgency of tasks.

Trainers do many things other than conduct training-room activities and one-on-one coaching sessions. They need to be good at parceling out time for such other tasks as preparing for training events, record keeping, reporting to their supervisors, and so forth. Highly competent trainers are capable of "multitasking," of keeping goals and priorities clearly in focus as they carry out myriad responsibilities.

◆ **Motivate others:** Encourages others to achieve desired results. Creates enthusiasm and commitment in others.

Trainers cannot, of course, motivate coaches because coaches are already motivated. The task is to channel their motivation in productive ways so that trainees approach the task of learning how to be effective coaches with vigor and commitment. Newly appointed coaches usually want to learn how to cope with their new responsibilities, and trainers need to capitalize on that motivation by enrolling them in meaningful learning activities.

◆ **Teamwork:** Cooperates with others to achieve a common purpose.

This competency is vital in two ways. First, trainers often work together in preparing coaches, and they need to be capable of authentically modeling teamwork within the training staff. Second, as this book emphasizes, efficient training usually involves learning teams. Trainers need to be highly capable of forming, structuring, instructing, and supporting the use of teams in the formal learning environment. Trainers need to be capable of helping groups become teams by committing to cooperative work toward commonly prized objectives.

◆ **Planning and organizing:** Takes a well-ordered and logical approach to organizing work and completing tasks.

Sloppy work habits generate haphazard training. Trainers who have the important responsibility of working with coaches must be capable of organizing their own work

*Continued on next page*

**Assessment 11–4, continued**

**Trainer Competencies**

as well as modeling this for trainees. Also, they need to be highly resourceful in working with such trainees to assist them in becoming and remaining organized.

Coaches can become overwhelmed with their responsibilities and relationships. Trainers need to work productively with them to avoid this happening by helping them stay on top of their jobs through planning.

◆ **Attention to detail:** Makes sure work is done correctly and completely.

Many organizations have explicit standards for training and measurements in place to monitor adherence to them. Training is not magic. There are effective and ineffective practices. It is vital that trainers pay close attention to learning what these are and meeting the needs of the organization and coaches consistently and well. This means making sure that the details of all work—and especially all training events—are planned and executed completely.

*Continued on next page*

## Assessment 11–4, continued
## Trainer Competencies

*Instructions:* If you are using this instrument as a self-assessment, write an **X** in the box to the right of each of the 12 trainer competencies that best describes your level of skill. If you are using this form to give feedback to a trainer, place an **X** in the box that best fits his or her level of competence in each area.

| COMPETENCY | ALMOST NONE IN THIS AREA | LITTLE IN THIS AREA | SOME IN THIS AREA | ADEQUATE IN THIS AREA | EXPERT IN THIS AREA |
|---|---|---|---|---|---|
| **Facilitation.** Leads group discussion without directing the outcome. Creates an environment of openness and trust. | ☐ | ☐ | ☐ | ☐ | ☐ |
| **Communication.** Speaks clearly and expresses self well in public settings. Conveys ideas in terms the listener can understand. | ☐ | ☐ | ☐ | ☐ | ☐ |
| **Listening.** Demonstrates attention to and conveys understanding of others. | ☐ | ☐ | ☐ | ☐ | ☐ |
| **Coaching.** Assesses strengths and weaknesses of others. Gives timely, specific, and constructive feedback. | ☐ | ☐ | ☐ | ☐ | ☐ |
| **Sensitivity to others.** Recognizes feelings, attitudes, and concerns of others. | ☐ | ☐ | ☐ | ☐ | ☐ |
| **Managing conflict.** Identifies sources of conflict. Uses conflict as a constructive process to exchange ideas. Keeps energy focused on desired outcomes. | ☐ | ☐ | ☐ | ☐ | ☐ |
| **Influence.** Persuades others to consider a desired point of view. Gains support and commitment from others. Effects change in behavior of others. | ☐ | ☐ | ☐ | ☐ | ☐ |
| **Time management.** Sets efficient work priorities. Can work on many tasks simultaneously. Balances importance and urgency of tasks. | ☐ | ☐ | ☐ | ☐ | ☐ |
| **Motivate others.** Encourages others to achieve desired results. Creates enthusiasm and commitment in others. | ☐ | ☐ | ☐ | ☐ | ☐ |
| **Teamwork.** Cooperates with others to achieve a common purpose. | ☐ | ☐ | ☐ | ☐ | ☐ |
| **Planning and organizing.** Takes a well-ordered and logical approach to organizing work and completing tasks. | ☐ | ☐ | ☐ | ☐ | ☐ |
| **Attention to detail.** Makes sure work is done correctly and completely. | ☐ | ☐ | ☐ | ☐ | ☐ |

## *Assessment 11–5*

## Coaching Training Follow-Up Assessment

*Instructions:* This form focuses on the outcomes of the training in which this coach recently participated. Please give your open and honest assessment of the person's current level of functioning. On the line to the left, write a number from 1 to 6 (based on the scale below) to rate the person on each of these 13 aspects of coaching.

| | |
|---|---|
| *Participant Code:* | |
| _____ | |

| | |
|---|---|
| 1 = HIGHLY INEFFECTIVE | 4 = SOMEWHAT EFFECTIVE |
| 2 = INEFFECTIVE | 5 = EFFECTIVE |
| 3 = A BIT INEFFECTIVE | 6 = HIGHLY EFFECTIVE |

_____ **Communicating instruction:** Showing how to accomplish a task and clarifying when, where, how much, and to what standard it should be done.

_____ **Setting performance goals:** Collaborating with others to establish short- and long-term goals for performance on particular tasks.

_____ **Providing feedback:** Carefully observing performance on individual tasks and sharing these observations in a nonthreatening manner.

_____ **Rewarding improvement:** Using a variety of means to provide positive reinforcement to others for making progress on the accomplishment of important tasks.

_____ **Dealing with failure:** Working with others to encourage them when they do not meet expectations.

_____ **Working with personal issues:** Listening empathically and without judgment, and offering emotional support for nonwork difficulties.

_____ **Confronting difficult situations:** Raising uncomfortable topics that are affecting task accomplishment.

_____ **Responding to requests:** Consulting with others on an as-needed basis. Responding to requests in a timely manner.

_____ **Following through:** Keeping commitments. Monitoring outcomes of the coaching process and providing additional assistance when necessary.

_____ **Listening for understanding:** Demonstrating attention to and conveying understanding of others.

_____ **Motivating others:** Encouraging others to achieve desired results. Creating enthusiasm and commitment in others.

_____ **Assessing strengths and weaknesses:** Identifying root causes of individual performance. Probing beneath the surface of problems. Keenly observing people and events. Defining and articulating issues effectively.

_____ **Building rapport and trust:** Showing respect for others. Acting with integrity and honesty. Easily building bonds with others. Making others feel their concerns and contributions are important.

## Assessment 11–6
## Coaching Needs Assessment

**Instructions:** Use this assessment to determine the most important coaching needs of the person you are coaching. You should complete the assessment based on discussions with the person you are coaching, his or her supervisor (if applicable), and your own observations.

| DOES THE PERSON YOU ARE COACHING: | TO A GREAT EXTENT | FOR THE MOST PART | TO SOME EXTENT | NOT AT ALL |
|---|---|---|---|---|
| 1. Have a high level of commitment to the task or responsibility? | ☐ | ☐ | ☐ | ☐ |
| 2. Have a clear understanding of his or her role in the organization? | ☐ | ☐ | ☐ | ☐ |
| 3. Have clearly defined tasks or responsibilities? | ☐ | ☐ | ☐ | ☐ |
| 4. Have a clear understanding of what it means to be successful regarding those tasks or responsibilities? | ☐ | ☐ | ☐ | ☐ |
| 5. Have an awareness of positive consequences that will result from success and negative consequences that will result from failure? | ☐ | ☐ | ☐ | ☐ |
| 6. Have a firm belief that he or she can accomplish or handle the task or responsibility? | ☐ | ☐ | ☐ | ☐ |
| 7. Find the task or responsibility interesting or enjoyable? | ☐ | ☐ | ☐ | ☐ |
| 8. Have a plan to accomplish the task or fulfill the responsibility? | ☐ | ☐ | ☐ | ☐ |
| 9. Possess the skills to accomplish or fulfill the task or responsibility? | ☐ | ☐ | ☐ | ☐ |
| 10. Possess the knowledge necessary to accomplish or fulfill the task or responsibility? | ☐ | ☐ | ☐ | ☐ |
| 11. Have a natural inclination toward or aversion to the task or responsibility? | ☐ | ☐ | ☐ | ☐ |
| 12. Have a well-defined career path? | ☐ | ☐ | ☐ | ☐ |
| 13. Understand his or her career interests? | ☐ | ☐ | ☐ | ☐ |
| 14. Have a good understanding of the culture and norms of the organization? | ☐ | ☐ | ☐ | ☐ |

*Continued on next page*

## *Assessment 11–6, continued*
## *Coaching Needs Assessment*

The results of this assessment can help direct and focus your coaching efforts. They can also help you determine the nature of your coaching role (guide, teacher, motivator, mentor). The roles are not exclusive, but low ratings (to some extent, not at all) on certain items can indicate which role(s) are most needed.

- ◆ Low ratings on items 2, 3, 4, and 8 indicate a need for the coach to act as a guide.
- ◆ Low ratings on items 9 and 10 indicate a need for the coach to act as a teacher.
- ◆ Low ratings on items 1, 5, 6, 7, and 11 indicates a need for the coach to act as a motivator. A high rating on item 6 may also indicate an issue with overconfidence.
- ◆ A low rating on items 2, 3, 12, 13, and 14 indicate a need for the coach to act as a mentor.

## *Assessment 11–7*
**Listening Self-Assessment**

***Instructions:*** This assessment will help you identify ways to improve your listening skills. Write an **X** in one of the boxes to the right of each statement, depending on how often you behave as described in the statement. Obviously, you need to be honest with yourself on this. No one will see your ratings unless you voluntarily share them.

| LISTENING BEHAVIOR | ALWAYS | MOST OF THE TIME | SOMETIMES | RARELY | NEVER |
|---|---|---|---|---|---|
| **When another person is speaking to me, I . . .** | | | | | |
| 1. Make eye contact with the person. | ☐ | ☐ | ☐ | ☐ | ☐ |
| 2. Think of different perspectives I have on the same topic. | ☐ | ☐ | ☐ | ☐ | ☐ |
| 3. Rephrase the comments and ideas back to the other person. | ☐ | ☐ | ☐ | ☐ | ☐ |
| 4. Try to anticipate what the person will say next. | ☐ | ☐ | ☐ | ☐ | ☐ |
| 5. Pay attention to his or her facial expression, hand gestures, posture, and other physical cues. | ☐ | ☐ | ☐ | ☐ | ☐ |
| 6. Think about issues not related to the conversation. | ☐ | ☐ | ☐ | ☐ | ☐ |
| 7. Think about what I am going to say next. | ☐ | ☐ | ☐ | ☐ | ☐ |
| 8. Interrupt to make a point or comment. | ☐ | ☐ | ☐ | ☐ | ☐ |
| 9. Prepare a response to a prior comment. | ☐ | ☐ | ☐ | ☐ | ☐ |
| 10. Smile, nod, or give other physical cues in response. | ☐ | ☐ | ☐ | ☐ | ☐ |
| 11. Ask follow-up or probing questions to gain clarity or get more information. | ☐ | ☐ | ☐ | ☐ | ☐ |
| 12. Immediately react emotionally to the message. | ☐ | ☐ | ☐ | ☐ | ☐ |

*Continued on next page*

### Assessment 11–7, continued
### Listening Self-Assessment

The results of this assessment can help direct and focus your efforts to improve your listening skills. This assessment considers how adept you are at three aspects of effective listening: focus, feedback, and filtering.

+ **Focus:** Being attentive to the speaker and the message he or she is trying to convey.
+ **Feedback:** Completing the communication cycle by encouraging the speaker, asking clarifying questions, paraphrasing statements, and summarizing key points.
+ **Filtering:** Creating personal meaning from the speaker's comments. Putting the speaker's comments in context with your own experiences, knowledge, and perceptions.

If you scored yourself more toward the "Always" column on questions 6, 7, and 9, or toward the "Never" column on questions 1 and 5, you may need to work on your focus when listening to others.

If you scored yourself more toward the "Always" column on questions 8 or toward the "Never" column on questions 3, 10, and 11, you may need to work on how effectively you provide feedback when listening to others.

If you scored yourself more toward the "Always" column on questions 2, 4, and 12, you may need to work on how you filter information when listening to others.

*Training Instrument 11–1*
**Coaching Agreements Worksheet**

I am the *(check one):*

☐ Coach

☐ Person being coached

**Personal Success Statement**

I will consider this coaching engagement a personal success if I . . . *(for example, am promoted or learn to use the new computer system)*

**Commitment Statement**

To achieve my personal success statement, I will . . .

**Expectations Statement**

To help me achieve my personal success statement, I expect you to . . .

*Training Instrument 11–2*

**Feedback Preparation Worksheet**

Feedback for: _____

Situation:

Behavior:

Impact:

*Training Instrument 11–3*

**Process Steps Worksheet**

*Instructions:* List the inputs required to complete the task or process (use another sheet of paper if more inputs are required).

1. _____

2. _____

3. _____

4. _____

5. _____

*Instructions:* List the results of the completed task or process (use another sheet of paper if more results are produced).

1. _____

2. _____

3. _____

4. _____

5. _____

*Instructions:* List the process steps required to complete the task or process (use another sheet of paper if more steps are required).

1. _____

2. _____

3. _____

4. _____

5. _____

6. _____

7. _____

8. _____

9. _____

10. _____

---

*Training Instrument 11–4*

## Values Worksheet

*Instructions:* In column 1 rank the values in order of their importance to you, from 1 through 19. (The most important value to you should be ranked 1 and the least important 19.) When ranking values it might be helpful to ask yourself, "If I had to choose between fulfilling these values, which would I fulfill?"

When you have completed column 1, the facilitator will provide instructions for column 2.

|  | 1 | 2 |
|---|---|---|
| **Achievement** (sense of accomplishment, reaching goals, facing challenges) | ☐ | ☐ |
| **Adventure** (new, different, and exciting experiences) | ☐ | ☐ |
| **Career** (success in the workplace, promotions, titles) | ☐ | ☐ |
| **Compassion** (caring for the wants and needs of others) | ☐ | ☐ |
| **Fairness** (sense of justice, adherence to principles) | ☐ | ☐ |
| **Faith** (having a relationship with a higher power, religious belief) | ☐ | ☐ |
| **Family** (close relationships with those related to you) | ☐ | ☐ |
| **Freedom** (independence, autonomy, ability to make choices) | ☐ | ☐ |
| **Friendship** (close, positive, personal relationships with others) | ☐ | ☐ |
| **Happiness** (emotional contentment, joy, personal peace) | ☐ | ☐ |
| **Health** (physical and mental well-being) | ☐ | ☐ |
| **Integrity** (honesty, sincerity, standing up for beliefs) | ☐ | ☐ |
| **Loyalty** (duty, commitment to obligation, allegiance) | ☐ | ☐ |
| **Power** (authority, control of resources, influence over others) | ☐ | ☐ |
| **Responsibility** (accountability for consequences of behavior) | ☐ | ☐ |
| **Self-respect** (pride, sense of personal identity) | ☐ | ☐ |
| **Stability** (order, permanence, lack of change) | ☐ | ☐ |
| **Status** (prestige, admiration of others) | ☐ | ☐ |
| **Wealth** (accumulating money and financial resources) | ☐ | ☐ |

# Structured Experiences

- Explanation of structured experiences

- Step-by-step instructions for using structured experiences

- Twelve structured experiences

This chapter contains 12 structured experiences to assist in the learning process. A structured experience is a step-by-step design that implements the Experiential Learning Cycle. Each experience includes

- **Goals:** The learning outcomes that the experience is designed to achieve.

- **Materials:** A listing of all materials required to facilitate the experience.

- **Time:** Anticipated time allowances for each step of the experience. These can vary based on the facilitator and the participants.

- **Instructions:** Step-by-step instructions to facilitate the experience.

- **Debriefing:** Suggested debriefing topics and questions. These should be modified to meet the needs of the participants.

## The Structured Experiences

Each of the following designs is self-contained. Although some of the experiences are designed specifically for learning outcomes associated with the module they support, others can be used in a variety of modules that the trainer either presently uses or is developing.

◆ **Structured Experience 12–1: What Is Coaching?** This structured experience involves a role-play that helps participants explore the various ways a coach interacts with the person being coached. It is a part of the "What Is Coaching?" content module.

◆ **Structured Experience 12–2: I Want to Drive.** This is a negotiation exercise based on a context to which almost everyone can relate. It is used in the "Needs Assessment and Defining the Coaching Relationship" content module.

◆ **Structured Experience 12–3: Building Rapport.** This is an introspective and interactive experience in which participants discover commonalities among themselves. It is included in the "Building Trust and Rapport" content module.

◆ **Structured Experience 12–4: Trust Walk.** This is a well-known exercise that explores the issue of trust. It is used in the "Building Trust and Rapport" content module.

◆ **Structured Experience 12–5: Draw It.** This is a communication exercise that looks at the differences in effectiveness between one-way and two-way communication. It is part of the "Listening for Understanding" content module.

◆ **Structured Experience 12–6: Team Theater.** This is a fun and energizing exercise that provides participants feedback observation opportunities with the other participants. It is used in the "Giving Effective Feedback" content module.

◆ **Structured Experience 12–7: Where Do I Want to Go?** This experience includes a visioning exercise. It provides coaches with a process to guide others through the personal visioning process. It supports the "Coach as Guide" content module.

◆ **Structured Experience 12–8: Break It Down.** In this exercise participants create a step-by-step breakdown of a process with which they are familiar. It is part of the "Coach as Teacher" content module.

◆ **Structured Experience 12–9: Origami Knowledge Transfer.** Participants learn how to make a simple origami figure and then try to teach this skill to another participant. An insightful exercise with tangible results. It is used in the "Coach as Teacher" content module.

- **Structured Experience 12–10: Snowflake.** Participants work in a group to create a "snowflake" with paper and scissors and then create instructions to help another participant replicate the snowflake. It is used in the "Coach as Teacher" content module for large groups.

- **Structured Experience 12–11: What's Important to Me?** This experience explores the power of understanding values in motivating others. It includes a values ranking exercise and supports the content module "Coach as Motivator."

- **Structured Experience 12–12: Mentoring Discussion.** This is a structured discussion and interactive learning experience on adding value as a mentor. It is part of the "Coach as Mentor" content module.

# Structured Experience 12–1: What Is Coaching?

## *GOALS*

The goals of this experience are to

- ◆ allow participants to interact with and learn from each other

- ◆ explore different aspects of the coaching process.

## *MATERIALS*

None

## *TIME*

- ◆ 5 minutes for setup and introduction of exercise

- ◆ 15 minutes for small group discussion

- ◆ 10 minutes for debriefing

## *INSTRUCTIONS*

1. Divide participants into groups of three or four.

2. Tell participants they have just taken on the role of personal fitness coach. Their client's goal is to lose weight. They've already told their client to "eat less and exercise."

3. Ask participants to brainstorm other things they might do in their role as coach. Allow 15 minutes for participants to brainstorm. Provide a time update when two minutes remain.

## *DEBRIEFING*

- ◆ Ask participants to share some of the ideas they came up with. Lead the debriefing into a discussion of how their ideas tie into the various coaching roles (guide, motivator, teacher, mentor). (10 minutes)

## Structured Experience 12–2: I Want to Drive

### GOALS

The goals of this experience are to

◆ explore the two-way nature of the coaching relationship

◆ teach participants to align expectations with the person they are coaching by using Training Instrument 11–1: Coaching Agreements Worksheet (chapter 11, page 141)

◆ emphasize the importance of aligned expectations between the coach and the person being coached.

### MATERIALS

The materials needed for this structured experience are

◆ Copies of Training Instrument 11–1: Coaching Agreements Worksheet.

### TIME

◆ 5 minutes for set-up

◆ 30 minutes for role-play

◆ 25 minutes for debriefing

### INSTRUCTIONS

1. Divide participants into pairs. Provide each person with a copy of the training instrument.

2. Explain to participants that they will be participating in a role-playing exercise. One of them will be a teenager who wants to learn how to drive. The other will be the teenager's parent. Ask each pair to select who will play each role.

3. Explain that the teenager is the person being coached and the parent is the coach. Ask participants to draft a personal success statement on their worksheets. Give them up to 5 minutes if needed.

**4.** When they have completed their success statements, have each person review his or her partner's statement. They may ask for clarifications, but are not allowed to suggest revisions.

**5.** When they have completed their reviews, have them complete the commitment and expectations statements. Give them up to 5 minutes.

**6.** Ask them to take turns responding to the other's expectations statements. Tell them they can respond to each expectation statement with "I will," "I will if . . . ," or "I will not because. . . . "

**7.** Have the participants modify their expectations statements if necessary until both the parent and teenager have come to an agreement on expectations or time has run out. Allow 20 minutes for negotiations.

### *DEBRIEFING*

**1.** Have the participants take turns discussing the following questions in their pairs. Ask each pair to identify three ways to negotiate effective roles (15 minutes).

- Were the success statements clear?

- Did knowing your partner's success statement help you come to agreement on expectations? Why or why not?

- Were the expectations initially reasonable?

- Did your negotiations help you better understand your partner's point of view?

- Did you attempt to create balance between what you committed to and what you expected from the other person?

- What hindered negotiations?

- What helped negotiations?

**2.** Have each pair share the three ways they identified to negotiate effective roles (10 minutes).

## Structured Experience 12–3: Building Rapport

### GOALS

The goals of this experience are to

◆ reinforce the fact that most people share many similarities

◆ demonstrate the power of focusing on similarities instead of differences

◆ build rapport and relationships among participants.

### MATERIALS

None

### TIME

◆ 10 minutes for setup, brainstorming, and prioritizing

◆ 30 minutes for similarity networking session

◆ 20 minutes for debriefing

### INSTRUCTIONS

1. Ask participants to brainstorm and write down all the different ways they identify themselves or others identify them (that is, the roles they play). Examples are father, wife, athlete, christian, engineer, stamp collector, baseball fan, investor, or video game junkie. Have them write down all that come to mind.

2. When they have completed their lists (about 5 minutes), ask them to pick the five items that are most important or have the most meaning for them. Remind them that these are not necessarily where they spend the most time.

3. When they have completed their priorities have them stand up, walk around the room, and network with others. Their goal is to find another person with the same roles in their top five. As they find their top five role matches, ask them to spend a few moments discussing with each other why those roles are important to them.

4. After 30 minutes, ask participants to return to their seats.

### *DEBRIEFING*

Allow approximately 20 minutes for the debriefing.

1.  Ask if anyone found someone else with the same top five roles. Were they surprised?

2.  Ask if people were surprised at the number of matches they found with other people or if they found an unexpected commonality with someone.

3.  Ask participants to reflect on how it felt to discuss a commonly prioritized role.

4.  Explore how the discovery and discussion of similarities helps to build rapport between people.

# Structured Experience 12–4: Trust Walk

## GOALS

The goals of this experience are to

- explore the dynamics of building trust

- teach participants to gain the trust of others

- build trust among participants.

## MATERIALS

The materials needed for this structured experience are

- blindfolds for all participants (cloth bandannas work well).

## TIME

- 5 minutes for setup

- 20 minutes for walks

- 20 minutes for debriefing

## INSTRUCTIONS

1. Divide participants into pairs. Provide each person with a blindfold.

2. Ask one person in each pair to volunteer to wear his or her blindfold. Have the volunteers put their blindfolds on.

3. When they have put their blindfolds on, tell participants that they will be taking a walk around the training facility. The sighted partners will guide the blindfolded participants. Tell them they can walk wherever they would like, but *the sighted partners are responsible for the safety of their blindfolded partners*. Emphasize this point because some may not take it seriously. They have 10 minutes for their walk. After 10 minutes, the sighted person will put on his or her blindfold, the blindfolded person will remove his or hers, and they will switch roles. This walk should end in 10 minutes back in the training room.

4. As the pairs return, have them remove their blindfolds and begin the debriefing.

### *DEBRIEFING*

1.  Have the participants take turns discussing the following questions in their pairs. Ask each pair to identify three ways to build trust (15 minutes).

    ◆ When you first started your walk blindfolded, how much did you trust your partner to guide you safely? Why?

    ◆ What did your sighted partner do that increased your level of trust?

    ◆ What did your sighted partner do that decreased your level of trust?

    ◆ When you were guiding your blindfolded partner, to what extent did you consider how much they trusted you to guide them?

    ◆ Did you purposely take any actions to increase their trust in you?

    ◆ If you did, do you think your actions were effective? Why?

2.  Have each pair share the three ways they identified to build trust (5 minutes).

# Structured Experience 12–5: Draw It

## GOALS

The goals of this experience are to

- teach participants the importance of active listening

- allow participants to practice effective communication behaviors

- explore the differences between one-way and two-way communication.

## MATERIALS

The materials needed for this structured experience are

- writing instruments

- blank paper for drawing

- one copy of Handout 12–1 and Handout 12–2 (pages 157 and 158) for each pair of participants.

## TIME

- 5 minutes for setup and instructions

- 15 minutes to complete and review diagram 1

- 15 minutes to complete and review diagram 2

- 25 minutes for debriefing

## INSTRUCTIONS

1. Divide participants into pairs. If there is an odd number of participants, allow one group of three.

2. Have one person in each pair or trio volunteer to be the "speaker." The remaining person(s) is/are the "listener(s)." Have the speakers arrange their chairs so they sit back-to-back with the listener(s).

3. Provide each speaker with a copy of diagram 1 and ensure that each listener has paper and a writing instrument. Make sure the listeners do not see the diagram.

4. Address the group as follows: "The speakers are going to describe a diagram to their listeners. Based on this description, the listeners are

to recreate the diagram on their paper. Listeners are not allowed to speak or make any other noise."

5.  Ask the speakers to being describing their diagram to their listeners. Remind listeners not to make any noise. Tell them they have 12 minutes to complete their diagrams.

6.  After 12 minutes has passed, ask listeners to compare their diagrams with the diagrams of the speakers. If pairs finish their diagrams early, they may start this process as soon as they have finished.

7.  After pairs have had a couple of minutes to compare their diagrams ask them to set aside their diagrams and take their back-to-back positions again.

8.  Tell them they will try to recreate another diagram, but this time the listener may ask questions of the speaker during the exercise.

9.  Hand out diagram 2 and ask the pairs to begin.

10. After 12 minutes have passed, ask listeners to compare their diagrams with the diagrams of the speakers. If pairs finish their diagrams early, they may start this process as soon as they have finished.

### *DEBRIEFING*

Debrief as a group using the questions below. The theme to elicit is the impact of active listening on the speaker and listener and its impact on the effectiveness of communications (approximately 25 minutes).

1.  How did the speakers feel while giving instructions on diagram 1? How did the speakers feel while giving instructions on diagram 2?

2.  How did the listeners feel while receiving instructions on diagram 1? How did the listeners feel while receiving instructions on diagram 2?

3.  How did the recreations of diagram 1 compare with those of diagram 2?

4.  What are the advantages and disadvantages of one-way communication (passive listening)?

5.  What are the advantages and disadvantages of two-way communication (active listening)?

*Handout 12–1*

**Draw It Diagram 1**

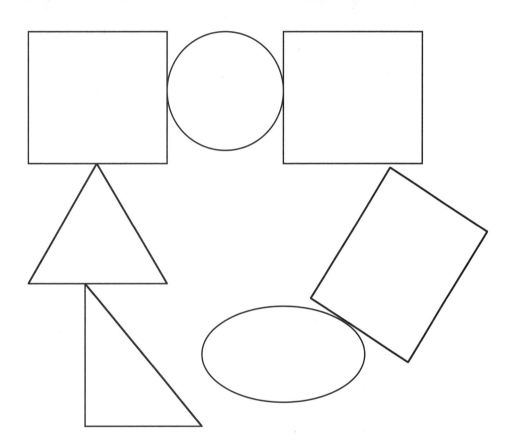

## Handout 12–2
### Draw It Diagram 2

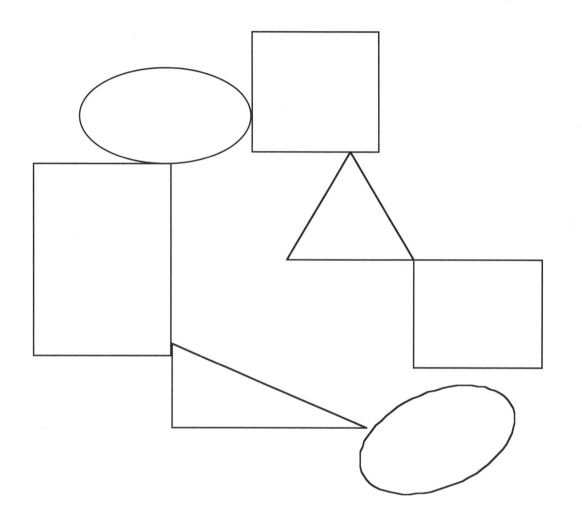

1.  Did using the situation-behavior-impact model make it easier to give feedback?

2.  Was it hard to avoid using judgmental terms, such as "good" and "bad" when giving feedback?

3.  Was the feedback you received helpful?

## Structured Experience 12–7: Where Do I Want to Go?

### GOALS

The goals of this experience are to

- help participants understand how to help someone create a personal vision and associated goals

- provide participants with a process to help others create personal visions and goals.

### MATERIALS

For this structured experience participants will need writing materials and paper.

### TIME

- 15 minutes for setup and vision development

- 30 minutes for paired discussions

- 15 minutes for debriefing

### INSTRUCTIONS

1. Ask participants to think of and write down what changes would dramatically improve the quality of their lives.

2. Ask each participant to craft a statement describing his or her dramatically improved life (a personal vision statement describing a desired future state).

3. Ask participants to write down three specific things that need to be different than they are today to help make the vision a reality.

4. When participants have finished, ask them to write down three more things that need to be different than today to help make those changes a reality.

5. Have each participant select a partner. Instruct each pair to take turns reviewing each other's personal vision and changes required, and suggesting short-term goals that would help achieve the vision. Have them pay particular attention to the following issues:

- ◆  **Creative tension:** How different is the future vision from the current state?

- ◆  **Ability to influence:** How much control do they have over the likelihood that the required changes will take place?

- ◆  **Obstacles:** What potential obstacles are there to achieving their visions?

6.  Allow 30 minutes for the discussion. Halfway into the time allotted, remind them to be good time managers and allow each person the opportunity for discussion.

## *DEBRIEFING*

Debrief as a group using the topics below (approximately 15 minutes).

1.  Was it easy or difficult to create a personal vision? Why?

2.  Was it easy or difficult to assist your partner in identifying short-term goals? Why?

3.  What obstacles might you encounter when helping someone you are coaching develop a vision and set goals? What can you do to overcome them?

# Structured Experience 12–8: Break It Down

## GOALS

The goals of this experience are to

- teach participants to define and articulate discrete steps in a process

- enable participants to practice effective coaching behaviors

- explore the process of instructing another person in a skill that is second nature to you.

## MATERIALS

For this structured experience you will need copies of Training Instrument 11–3: Process Steps Worksheet for each participant.

## TIME

- 15 minutes for setup and completing the worksheet

- 30 minutes for clarification coaching session

- 15 minutes for debriefing

## INSTRUCTIONS

1. Ask participants to think of a task or process with which they are familiar and proficient.

2. Introduce the Process Steps Worksheet. Explain that the participants are to list the inputs and outputs to the task or process and the steps required to complete the task or process.

3. Allow 10 minutes for participants to complete the worksheet. Provide a time update when two minutes remain.

4. Have each participant select a partner to work with. Instruct each pair to take turns reviewing each other's Process Steps Worksheet and explore the following issues:

   - Is the worksheet clear enough to allow someone unfamiliar with the task/process to complete the task/process?

◆ How could the worksheet be more readily understandable, useful, and complete to someone unfamiliar with the task or process?

5. Allow 30 minutes for the discussion. Halfway into the time allotted, remind them to be good time managers and allow each person the opportunity for feedback.

## DEBRIEFING

Debrief as a group using the topics below (approximately 15 minutes).

1. Was it easy or difficult to identify the inputs, outputs, and process steps of a task or process with which you are familiar?

2. How easy or difficult was it for another person to understand the inputs, outputs, and process steps you identified?

3. Did your partner's perspective on your list of steps differ from yours or help you clarify the steps you take?

# Structured Experience 12–9: Origami Knowledge Transfer

## GOALS

The goals for this experience are to

- teach participants to coach another person through a complex process

- allow participants to practice effective teaching behaviors

- explore the process of instructing another person in a complex process.

## MATERIALS

For this structured experience you will need

- square pieces of paper (enough for three sheets for each participant) For folding, 8.5 × 8.5 inches works well and is easily cut from an 8.5 × 11–inch piece of paper.

- Handout 12–3: Swan Origami Instructions and Handout 12–4: Frog Origami Instructions. Photos depicting the folding of the Swan origami appear only on the accompanying CD.

## TIME

- 5 minutes for setup

- 10 minutes for origami practice session

- 20 minutes for teaching session

- 25 minutes for debriefing

## INSTRUCTIONS

1.  Divide participants into pairs. (As an option, you can add an observer to each pair. During the debriefing the observer would add his or her comments on the effectiveness or ineffectiveness of the instruction process.)

2.  Give one person in each pair a Swan instruction sheet and the other person a Frog instruction sheet.

3. Tell the pairs the person with the Swan sheet (the coach) will be instructing his or her partner (the learner) on how to create the swan. The instructions will be verbal only. The coach is not allowed to show the learner any visual aids, including the instruction sheet, and may not use hand gestures or touch the materials or the learner.

4. Split the pairs up so each person is physically separated from his or her partner. Tell them this time is for the coach to become familiar with the swan creation process and for the leaner to practice his or her origami skills with the Frog sheet.

5. Allow 10 minutes for participants to practice creating the origami figure on their instruction sheets. The facilitator can help the coaches with their swan figures so they are as proficient as possible at creating their origami.

6. At the end of the practice period, bring the pairs back together.

7. Following the rules outlined in step 3, have the coaches teach the learners to create the swan figure. Allow 20 minutes for the teaching process.

## DEBRIEFING

Start the debriefing (approximately 25 minutes) by asking the coaches to discuss their experiences. Issues to explore include

1. What did you think was effective or ineffective in your coaching approach?

2. Was it difficult being limited to verbal instructions? How is this similar to coaching situations you might encounter?

3. Did you try to see the situation from the learner's perspective?

4. What was the attitude of the learner (eager, bored, frustrated)?

5. How did the learner's attitude affect the coaching process?

6. Were you tempted to blame the learner for poor results?

Have the learners discuss their experiences. Issues to explore include

1. What was effective or ineffective in the coach's teaching efforts?

2. Did the coach establish a common point of reference with you for instructions?

3. Did the coach attempt to describe the finished product you were creating?

4. Did the coach attempt to do some of the steps for you?

5. What was the attitude of the coach (frustrated, patient, not engaged)?

6. How did the coach's attitude affect your learning process?

Allow the coaches to respond to the learner's comments. Close by asking for lessons learned from the exercise.

## Handout 12–3
### Swan Origami Instructions

1.  Orient the paper in a diamond position.

2.  Bring the top point down to the bottom point to form a triangle.

3.  Bring the right point over to the left point to make a smaller triangle.

4.  With the opening facing you lift the top piece of paper and insert your finger to the back point of the triangle.

5.  As you do this, one point of the triangle lifts off the table. Simultaneously lift and shift this point to the opposite corner and squash it down, thus forming a square.

6.  Turn the paper over. You will see the outline of a triangle. Lift the extended point of the triangle until the triangle is perpendicular to the square base.

7.  Hold the square down with one hand and open the triangle with the other. Again, insert your finger to the back point of the triangle. As you do this, the uppermost point begins to draw downward. Remove your finger and draw the point down to squash and form another square.

8.  With the opening facing you, lift the first layers of paper at the lower right and left edges and bring them to the centerfold to form a kite shape. Turn over and repeat.

9.  Fold the top triangle of the kite down over the lower kite shape that you just folded. Do this back and forth, then unfold to return to the kite shape.

10. Now hold down the small triangle at the top and unfold the right and left flaps. Continue to hold down the triangle as you lift the first layer of paper. As you lift you will notice the sides turning inward, reversing the folds on the kite.

11. Open all the way to complete the reversing process. In front of you is a diamond shape with a seam up the middle. Turn over and repeat.

12. Examine the diamond. One end has two "legs." Narrow these legs by bringing the outer edge to the center. Turn over and repeat. You have just folded the neck and tail.

13. Pick your origami up off the table and lift the leg points up as far as they will go, and pull outward to form a "V."

14. Drop a leg down and gently unfold at the long (vertical) seam.

*Continued on next page*

## Handout 12–3, continued
**Swan Origami Instructions**

15. Place a finger at the short (horizontal) seam. And gently bring the narrow "leg" back upward so that it is now between the wing section. Reverse the fold on this part. Repeat.

16. Crimp fold one of the narrow points to form a head. You can also fold the wing tips down.

*Handout 12–4*

**Frog Origami Instructions**

1. Start with a square piece of paper. Fold the opposite edges together, then unfold. Repeat using the other edges. Open it up into a square again.

2. Fold each of the four corners to the center point.

3. Fold each of the two top edges to the center line.

4. Fold the triangle at the bottom upward.

5. Fold each of the bottom two corners to the middle of the bottom edge.

6. Fold the bottom portion upward (along the dotted line).

7. Fold the top half of the lower rectangle downward toward yourself. This forms the frog's legs.

8. Give your frog a head by folding a small part of the upper point downward. Draw two eyes, and your frog is done. To make your frog jump, push down where the "X" appears in diagram 8 and slide your finger away from the frog.

1.
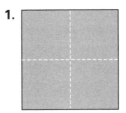

2.
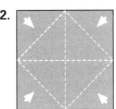

3.
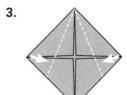

4.

5.
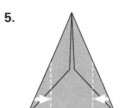

6.
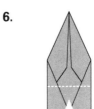

7.
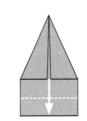

8.
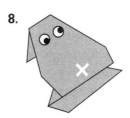

# Structured Experience 12–10: Snowflake

## GOALS

The goals of this experience are to

- teach participants to transfer process knowledge effectively

- explore the strengths and weaknesses of written instructions

- teach participants to create effective, step-by-step instructions in a group setting.

## MATERIALS

The materials needed for this structured experience are

- paper

- scissors

- pens or pencils

- prizes.

## TIME

- 5 minutes for setup

- 15 minutes to design a snowflake and write instructions for replicating it

- 10 minutes for volunteer to recreate snowflake

- 5 minutes for selecting the best snowflake and awarding prizes

- 25 minutes for debriefing.

## INSTRUCTIONS

1.  Organize participants into groups of five to eight people. Ask for one volunteer from each group. This volunteer will be the observer for the group.

2.  Ask for a second volunteer. This volunteer (the snowflake manufacturer) will try to recreate the snowflake design.

3.  Read these instructions to the participants:

"The first step of this exercise is for each group of snowflake designers to design a paper snowflake by making cuts in a folded piece of paper. Snowflake designs will be judged by the criteria of complexity and aesthetic appeal. After each group has designed its snowflake and created a prototype, it will develop a set of written instructions for its snowflake manufacturer. The snowflake manufacturer will be outside of the room during the design phase. The manufacturer will attempt to recreate the original snowflake design using only the written instructions. No talking is allowed during the manufacturing phase. The winning team will be selected based on the similarity of the manufactured snowflake to the prototype and the aesthetic appeal and complexity of the snowflake design."

4. Ask the snowflake manufacturers to leave the room. Have them convene in another room and spend the design time discussing a relevant question, such as, "Who was the most effective teacher you ever had? Why?"

5. Provide paper and scissors to design teams. Tell them they have 15 minutes to design their snowflakes and write their instructions. Remind them that their designs will be judged for aesthetic appeal and complexity.

6. Ask observers to be completely silent during the design and manufacturing phases. They should take notes on how effective or ineffective the instructions were and how they could have been more effective.

7. After the design phase time limit is reached, invite the manufacturers to join their respective teams of designers and use their instructions to create the snowflake.

8. Manufacturers are only allowed to use the written instructions to create their snowflakes. No talking or other assistance is permitted.

9. At the end of the manufacturing time or when all snowflakes have been produced, have each team display its prototype snowflake alongside the manufactured snowflake.

10. Have all participants browse the snowflake displays and then have each team vote for one snowflake team based on the best design and replication.

11. Award prizes to the winning team.

### *DEBRIEFING*

Begin the debriefing in teams. Ask each team to identify three lessons learned from the exercise. Start the team debriefing by having the observers share their comments with the team they were observing. Then have the manufacturers comment on the process. Encourage teams to react to the observations by probing the observer and manufacturer for more information. Suggest they consider the following issues (this segment will take about 20 minutes):

1.  How does complexity of a task affect the effectiveness of written instructions?

2.  Did the design team underestimate the difficulty of the task and of writing the instructions?

3.  Did the design team and manufacturer have different perspectives on the effectiveness of the instructions?

4.  Did the design team provide the manufacturer with a mental or physical picture of the finished product or just give step-by-step instructions?

5.  What could the design team have done to make the instructions more effective for the manufacturer?

Close the exercise by having each team share its three lessons learned with the entire group (5 minutes).

# Structured Experience 12-11: What's Important to Me?

## GOALS

The goals of this experience are to

- ◆ help participants understand the process and power of prioritizing their values

- ◆ provide participants with a tool to help others prioritize values.

## MATERIALS

For this structured experience you will need a copy of Training Instrument 11-4: Values Worksheet for each participant.

## TIME

- ◆ 15 minutes for setup and completing the worksheet

- ◆ 30 minutes for paired discussions

- ◆ 15 minutes for debriefing.

## INSTRUCTIONS

1. Provide each participant with a copy of the Values Worksheet.

2. Ask participants to follow the instructions for completing column 1.

3. Allow 10 minutes for participants to complete the worksheet. Provide a time update when 2 minutes remain.

4. When participants have completed column 1, ask them to rate (on a scale of 1 to 5) how satisfied they are with the current fulfillment of their top 10 values (1 being completely unsatisfied and 5 being most satisfied). Instruct them to fill in their satisfaction ratings in column 2 on the worksheet.

5. Have each participant select a partner. Instruct each pair to take turns reviewing each other's Values Worksheet and explore the following issues:

    - ◆ How confident are they in their values rankings?

    - ◆ Do their current behaviors reflect the prioritization of their values?

◆ Which of their highly ranked values are not being satisfied?

◆ Focusing on the highest rated values with the lowest rated satisfaction, how might they change their behaviors to maximize their values satisfaction?

6. Allow 30 minutes for the discussion. Halfway into the time allotted, remind them to be good time managers and allow each person the opportunity for discussion.

## DEBRIEFING

Debrief as a group using the topics below. Allow approximately 15 minutes.

1. Was ranking values easy or did it require thought?

2. Was anyone surprised at the satisfaction level of some of their highly ranked values?

3. How can focusing on value importance and satisfaction motivate behavior?

## Structured Experience 12–12: Mentoring Discussion

### GOALS

The goals of this experience are to

◆ enable participants to interact with and learn from each other

◆ explore different aspects of the mentoring process.

### MATERIALS

No materials are needed for this structured experience.

### TIME

◆ 5 minutes for set-up and introducing the exercise

◆ 25 minutes for small group discussion

◆ 10 minutes for debriefing.

### INSTRUCTIONS

1. Divide participants into groups of three to four.

2. Ask participants to take turns answering the following questions. Encourage them to act as interviewers to draw out answers from their group members:

   ◆ What do you know now that you wish you knew early in your career? What difference would it have made?

   ◆ How could a mentor help you now?

   ◆ What lessons have you learned about working in our organization that you might pass on to someone else as his or her mentor?

### DEBRIEFING

Ask participants to share some of the ideas they came up with regarding how mentors can help their mentoring partners. Lead the debriefing into a discussion of how their ideas can make them effective mentors. Allow 10 minutes for this.

# Using the Compact Disc

Insert the CD and locate the file *How to Use This CD.txt*.

## Contents of the CD

The compact disc that accompanies this workbook on new employee orientation contains three types of files. All of the files can be used on a variety of computer platforms.

- **Adobe .pdf documents.** These include handouts, assessments, training instruments, and training tools.

- **Microsoft Word documents.** These text files can be edited to suit the specific circumstances of organizations and to fit the precise needs of trainers and trainees.

- **Microsoft PowerPoint presentations.** These presentations add interest and depth to many of the training activities included in the workbook.

- **Microsoft PowerPoint files of overhead transparency masters.** These files makes it easy to print viewgraphs and handouts in black-and-white rather than using an office copier. They contain only text and line drawings; there are no images to print in grayscale.

## Computer Requirements

To read or print the .pdf files on the CD, you must have Adobe Acrobat Reader software installed on your system. The program can be downloaded free of cost from the Adobe Website, *www.adobe.com*.

To use or adapt the contents of the PowerPoint presentation files on the CD, you must have Microsoft PowerPoint software installed on your system. If you simply want to view the PowerPoint documents, you must have an appropriate viewer installed on your system. Microsoft provides various viewers free for downloading from its Website, *www.microsoft.com*.

## Printing from the CD

### TEXT FILES

You can print the training materials using Adobe Acrobat Reader. Simply open the .pdf file and print as many copies as you need. The following documents can be directly printed from the CD:

- Assessment 11–1: Structured Interview Protocol for Assessing the Learning Needs of Coaches

- Assessment 11–2: Coaching Self-Assessment

- Assessment 11–3: Needs Assessment Focus Group Discussion Sheet

- Assessment 11–4: Trainer Competencies

- Assessment 11–5: Coaching Training Follow-Up Assessment

- Assessment 11–6: Coaching Needs Assessment

- Assessment 11–7: Listening Self-Assessment

- Training Instrument 11–1: Coaching Agreements Worksheet

- Training Instrument 11–2: Feedback Preparation Worksheet

- Training Instrument 11–3: Process Steps Worksheet

- Training Instrument 11–4: Values Worksheet

- Handout 12–1: Draw It Diagram 1

- Handout 12–2: Draw It Diagram 2

- Handout 12–3: Swan Origami Instructions

- Handout 12–4: Frog Origami Instructions

### *POWERPOINT SLIDES*

You can print the presentation slides directly from this CD using Microsoft PowerPoint. Simply open the .ppt files and print as many copies as you need. You can also make handouts of the presentations by printing 2, 4, or 6 "slides" per page. These slides will be in color, with design elements embedded. PowerPoint also permits you to print these in grayscale or black-and-white, although printing from the overhead masters file will yield better black-and-white representations. Many trainers who use personal computers to project their presentations bring along viewgraphs just in case there are glitches in the system.

## Adapting the PowerPoint Slides

You can modify or otherwise customize the slides by opening and editing them in the appropriate application. However, you must retain the denotation of the original source of the material—it is illegal to pass it off as your own work. You may indicate that a document was adapted from this workbook, written and copyrighted by Lou Russell and published by ASTD. The files will open as "Read Only," so before you adapt them you will need to save them onto your hard drive under a different filename.

## Showing the PowerPoint Presentations

On the CD, the following PowerPoint presentations are included:

- ◆ What Is Coaching.ppt
- ◆ Assessing Coaching Needs.ppt
- ◆ Defining the Coaching Relationship.ppt
- ◆ Building Trust & Rapport.ppt
- ◆ Listening for Understanding.ppt
- ◆ Effective Feedback.ppt
- ◆ Coach as Guide.ppt
- ◆ Coach as Teacher.ppt
- ◆ Coach as Motivator.ppt
- ◆ Coach as Mentor.ppt

### Table A–1
### Navigating Through a PowerPoint Presentation

| KEY | POWERPOINT "SHOW" ACTION |
| --- | --- |
| Space bar *or* Enter *or* Mouse click | Advance through custom animations embedded in the presentation |
| Backspace | Back up to the last projected element of the presentation |
| Escape | Abort the presentation |
| B *or* b | Blank the screen to black |
| B *or* b *(repeat)* | Resume the presentation |
| W *or* w | Blank the screen to white |
| W *or* w *(repeat)* | Resume the presentation |

Having the presentations in .ppt format means that it automatically shows full-screen when you double-click on its filename. You also can open Microsoft PowerPoint and launch it from there.

Use the space bar, the enter key, or mouse clicks to advance through a show. Press the backspace key to back up. Use the escape key to abort a presentation. If you want to blank the screen to black while the group discusses a point, press the B key. Pressing it again restores the show. If you want to blank the screen to a white background, do the same with the W key. Table A–1 summarizes these instructions.

We strongly recommend that trainers practice making presentations before using them in training situations. You should be confident that you can cogently expand on the points featured in the presentations and discuss the methods for working through them. If you want to engage your training participants fully (rather than worrying about how to show the next slide), become familiar with this simple technology *before* you need to use it. A good practice is to insert notes into the *Speaker's Notes* feature of the PowerPoint program, print them out, and have them in front of you when you present the slides.

# For Further Reading

Ambrose, Larry. *A Mentor's Companion*. Chicago, IL: Perrone-Ambrose Associates, Ltd., 1998.

Blanchard, Ken, and Don Shula. *The Little Book of Coaching: Motivating People to Be Winners*. New York: Harper Business, 2001.

Chen, Chris. *Simply Spoken Leadership*. Lancaster, PA: David and Roe Press, 1998.

Cottrell, David. *Monday Morning Leadership*. Dallas: Cornerstone Leadership Institute, 2002.

Covey, Stephen R. *The 7 Habits of Highly Effective People*. New York: Simon and Schuster, 1990.

Fournies, Ferdinand F. *Coaching for Improved Work Performance*. New York: McGraw-Hill, 1999.

Gebelein, Susan H., et al. *The Successful Manager's Handbook*. Minneapolis: Personnel Decisions, Inc., 1992.

Hargrove, Robert. *Masterful Coaching Fieldbook*. San Francisco, CA: Jossey-Bass, 1999.

Jones, John E. "Don't Smile about Smile Sheets." *Training & Development Journal*, December 1990.

Jones, John E., William L. Bearley, and Douglas C. Watsabaugh. *The New Fieldbook for Trainers: Tips, Tools, and Techniques*. Amherst, MA: HRD Press, 1996.

Jones, John E., and Chris Chen. *New Supervisor Training*. Alexandria, VA: American Society for Training & Development, 2002.

Jones, John E., and J. William Pfeiffer. *A Handbook of Structured Experiences for Human Relations Training*. San Diego, CA: Pfeiffer & Co., 1973.

Maxwell, John C. *Developing the Leaders around You*. Nashville: Thomas Nelson, 1995.

Rosener, Judy B. *America's Competitive Secret*. New York: Oxford University Press, 1995.

Senge, Peter, et al. *The Fifth Discipline Fieldbook*. New York: Doubleday, 1994.

Torres, Crescencio. *The Tao of Teams: A Guide to Team Success*. San Diego, CA: Pfeiffer & Co., 1994.

Zeus, Perry, and Suzanne Skiffington. *The Coaching at Work Toolkit: A Complete Guide to Techniques and Practices*. New York: McGraw-Hill, 2002.

**Chris W. Chen** is an organization effectiveness manager with Sempra Energy, a *Fortune* 500 company in San Diego, California. He also runs his own consulting business, specializing in leadership training. Previously, Chen led Sempra's organization development function, where he was responsible for leadership development, organization development, training, and employee communications. He held a similar role at the National Steel and Shipbuilding Company. While working for the Center for Creative Leadership, Chen was program manager for the Looking Glass Experience and Leading Downsized Organizations, and trained Foundations of Leadership and Leadership Development.

Before moving to San Diego, Chen spent 10 years as an organization effectiveness specialist in a high-technology *Fortune* 50 company. There he worked as a finance manager, human resource generalist, and organization development consultant. He has been responsible for conducting strategic needs assessments and preparing leadership development and succession plans for a 30,000-person organization, and has provided consulting in TQM, work design, team building, culture change, and performance management.

Chen has a bachelor of arts degree from the University of California, Irvine, where he majored in economics. He also received his master of business administration degree from UCI, where his studies included an emphasis in organizational behavior. He was an adjunct professor of organizational behavior at California State University, Long Beach, and lectured on TQM at the John Anderson Graduate School of Management (UCLA). His previous publications include *Simply Spoken Leadership* (David and Roe Press, 1998) and articles on a variety of human resource topics. He has spoken at several major conferences, including the Colby leadership conference.

# ASTD Press

## Delivering Training and Performance Knowledge You Will Use Today and Lead With Tomorrow

- Training Basics
- Evaluation / Return-on-Investment (ROI)
- E-Learning
- Instructional Systems Development (ISD)
- Leadership
- Career Development

**ASTD Press** is an internationally renowned source of insightful and practical information on workplace learning and performance topics, including training basics, evaluation and return-on-investment (ROI), instructional systems development (ISD), e-learning, leadership, and career development. You can trust that the books ASTD Press acquires, develops, edits, designs, and publishes meet the highest standards for accuracy and that our books reflect the most current industry practices. In addition, ASTD Press books are bottom-line oriented and geared toward immediate problem-solving application in the field.

**Ordering Information: Books published by ASTD Press can be purchased by visiting our website at store.astd.org or by calling 800.628.2783 or 703.683.8100.**